THE BEST DEVOTIONS OF

Barbara Johnson

WOMEN OF FAITH™

THE BEST DEVOTIONS OF

Barbara Johnson

ZONDERVAN™

GRAND RAPIDS, MICHIGAN 49530

ZONDERVAN™

The Best Devotions of Barbara Johnson
Copyright © 2001 by Barbara Johnson

Requests for information should be addressed to:

Zondervan, *Grand Rapids, Michigan 49530*

Library of Congress Cataloging-in-Publication Data

Johnson, Barbara (Barbara E.).
    The best devotions of Barbara Johnson/Barbara Johnson.
        p. cm.
    ISBN 0-310-24175-8
    1. Christian women—Prayer-books and devotions—English.
    I. Title.
    BV4844 .J635 2001
    242—dc21
                                      2001026579

All Scripture quotations, unless otherwise indicated, are from the *Holy Bible, New International Version* (NIV), © 1973, 1978, 1984 by the International Bible Society. Used by permission of Zondervan. All rights reserved.

Other Scripture quotations are from *The Message* (MSG), © 1993, 1994, 1995 by Eugene H. Peterson; *The Living Bible* (TLB), © 1971 by Tyndale House Publishers; *The New King James Version* (NKJV), © 1982 by Thomas Nelson, Inc., and the *King James Version* (KJV).

Published in association with the literary agency of Alive Communications, Inc., 7680 Goddard Street, Suite 200, Colorado Springs, CO 80920.

Interior design by Beth Shagene

Printed in the United States of America

---

01 02 03 04 05 06 07 08 /❖ DC/ 10 9 8 7 6 5 4 3 2 1

We want to hear from you. Please send your comments about this book to us in care of the address below. Thank you.

ZONDERVAN™

GRAND RAPIDS, MICHIGAN 49530

www.zondervan.com

To my porch pals—Patsy, Marilyn, Luci, Sheila,
and Thelma—who have helped me zoom
through the ups and downs of our joyful journey
with extravagant grace and boundless love.
Whenever dark clouds threaten to steal my joy,
I find the silver lining by remembering the
guffaws we've somehow tamed into giggles,
the candy we've sneaked from Mary's little black
bag, the silliness we've created at all times
and in all places—and the tears we've cried as
our hearts throbbed together in sympathy.
By now a million others know you as women
of faith, but I cherish you as heroes of hope.

Contents

Foreword by Thelma Wells *9*

Have You Checked Your Wardrobe Lately? *13*

Golden Moments *16*

Twenty-Five Ways to Make Your Day *19*

Forgiveness Means Get Over It *22*

No Strings Attached *25*

Be a Joy Germ *27*

Enjoy the Ride! *30*

The God Who Sees *33*

A Gift from the Scrap Pile *36*

Dot-to-Dot Living *39*

Bountiful Blessings *41*

The Most Powerful Perfume *44*

Encouraging Words *47*

Drunk Without Drinking *50*

Little Reminders *53*

Delightfully Deceived *56*

The Whole World in His Hands *59*

Never Cage Joy *62*

God's E-mail *65*

We're All Toads *68*

Grace-full in His Sight *71*

Singing in the Rain *74*

"Show Me the Love!" *77*

Love Everflowing *81*

Diamond Dust *84*

The Road to Hana *88*

Keep Sending Out Love *91*

Hooray for Gardening! *94*

God's Kingdom Fireworks *98*

Nestle, Don't Wrestle *101*

The Genius of Kids *105*

Unquenchable Grins *111*

Never Outgrow Motherhood *115*

Whatever, Lord! *119*

Love More and Regret Less *122*

The Boomerang Principle *124*

All My Marbles *128*

Birthday Countdown *133*

Making Life *Bearable* *137*

The Big Joy Room — In the Sky *139*

Crazy Quilt *144*

Spread Your Joy *147*

God's Spiritual Stove *150*

Waterproofing Life *153*

The Messages of Hands *157*

Anticipate the Best! *160*

Those Struggle Muscles *164*

Humble Joy *167*

God's Tear Bottle *170*

Gotcha! *173*

Prayer as Ointment *176*

Heir-Conditioning *179*

Season of Joy *182*

Hug-a-Day Club *185*

Scrapbooks of the Soul *188*

Living at Geriatric Junction *190*

Just a Little Hope *194*

Dream Big *197*

Merrymaking *201*

Blessed by Stress *205*

Foreword by Thelma Wells

I strolled into the speaker's room in Allentown, Pennsylvania, in 1996 for my debut with Women of Faith Conference and met a precious lady. My only previous connection to her was one of her books.

As we sat on the podium, she seemed quiet and undaunted by her surroundings. When she stood to speak, my ears perked up, my eyes widened, and the tears flowed. Her story was a modern day Job scenario. Why did all this happen to this lady? Who *is* this lady? What can I learn from her? Those questions were answered over the next five years.

Her husband, Bill, was in an accident that left him blind and convalescing for several years before God healed him. Five years apart to the day, Barbara identified the bodies of her oldest and second sons, who had both been killed tragically. That's a lot of grief!

One Father's Day weekend after his college graduation, her third son revealed his homosexuality. She reacted on horrified emotions that separated them for eleven years. That's a lot of rejection.

In early 2001 Barbara was diagnosed with a brain tumor. The surgery was successful, but the treatments continue.

Why did this happen to Barbara?

I can only speculate through Barbara's own words, "Everything that happens must go through God's filter."

Perhaps he allowed this because he knew he could trust her to carry these burdens with dignity, grace, and strength and help millions of others carry similar burdens. Just like God knew Job, he knows Barbara. Barbara proclaims with Job, "Though he slay me, yet will I trust in him."

Who is this lady?

Barbara is calm.

When the doctor told her he had the most disturbing news of her life, she commented, "He evidently doesn't know anything about my life." She calmly told me, "I have a brain tumor, which they will operate on, then I'll get some treatments, and I'll be back speaking." There was absolutely no agony in her voice. She was as cool as a cucumber.

Barbara is contagious.

With her dry humor and subtle wink, she twirls her first finger in the air making gestures and hums a three syllable "hum-hum-hum" and the room hoops with laughter. She instructs the audience, "Don't laugh: I don't have much more time. And besides, it wasn't good enough anyway," to which people laugh.

Barbara is a caretaker.

She's available to millions of hurting people worldwide through her ministry, Spatula Ministries. To her family, friends, and colleagues, she's a guardian angel. Every December, as a birthday present to herself, Barbara telephones and comforts people whose children have died within that year. At the conferences, she makes sure Mary Graham, the president of Women of Faith, eats properly by giving her lunches. And she makes sure I have all the big, decorative clip-on earrings I need to wear with my "stuff adorned" clothes.

Barbara Johnson is courageous!

It takes courage that only comes from a deep trust in God to pick up your husband from the road and watch a once happy and healthy man instantly become a near vegetable, to identify two sons in coffins, to survive a broken relationship with another son, and to hear you have a brain tumor. Through all of this, she maintains a bubble of joy in her heart. What courage!

What have I learned from Barbara?

With Barb, "What you see is what you get." Her complete disclosure of how she thinks, what she cares about, who she is, what her goals are, and what she says, leave no room to speculate about her realness. I've learned that authenticity is the true virtue of identity.

She has also taught me to look beyond profits and see other people's potential. But the greatest lesson I've learned from Barbara is to totally yield your heart to God. "Whatever, Lord" is her prayer of relinquishment. If that's not yielding, I don't know what is. She's telling God to have his way about everything in her life. For Barbara, this statement closed the portals of self-pity, loneliness, and depression, and she gained spiritual strength to become what she is to me and a bazillion of people everywhere.

Read the following pages and see if you don't agree about why, who, and what I've learned from Barbara Johnson. Better still, gather splashes of joy from the information, inspiration, and encouragement found in the practical life stories of the legendary and loving Barbara Johnson, the most applauded female Christian author on the planet.

Have You Checked Your Wardrobe Lately?

Therefore, as the elect of God, holy and beloved,
put on tender mercies, kindness, humility, meekness,
long-suffering; bearing with one another, and forgiving one
another . . . but above all these things put on love.
COLOSSIANS 3:12–14 NKJV

Like everybody else, I have to get up and get dressed every day. Too often I go to my closet and throw my hands in the air: "I don't have anything to wear!" My husband, Bill, shakes his head and laughs. "No really," I whine, peering into my closet and surveying the rod of hangers drooping with weight.

"This jacket is too worn," I say to myself. "It's got little fuzz balls all over it. This dress has gotten too small. That blouse hangs wrong at the shoulders; why did I let my sister talk me into buying it? This little number is totally outdated; I can't wear that. The blue sweater is the wrong color for my skin, and the pink one has a stain. Here's a good blouse, but I always feel frumpy in it. This one's uncomfortable; it chafes. This skirt is too long. This one's too short . . ."

I sit on the edge of my bed and pout: "Nothing to wear!" Bill is already back in the kitchen, oblivious to my dismay.

Seasons come and go. Clothing styles change. Different regions of my anatomy fluctuate in size. Fabrics wear thin, fade, and lose their appeal. Good thing I have another closet with unlimited choices. I have a wardrobe that will never fade, wear out, or go out of style. Best of all, these clothes fit perfectly each time I pull them out and put them on.

Have you checked your spiritual wardrobe lately? Recently a friend sent me a reminder about the apostle Paul's list describing the garments of the Holy Spirit in his letter to Colossian believers. First on his list is *tender mercies*. Also known as compassion, tender mercies are acts of empathy for weak or hurting people. They are usually motivated by feeling the same kind of pain as others or being able to imagine it. I call tender mercies the underwear of God's wardrobe — personal and next-to-the-skin. They are the foundation for everything that goes on the outside.

Next on Paul's list is *kindness.* Everyone can use a warmhearted deed as simple as a smile. But kindness is more than that. It is an attitude that becomes part of your lifestyle. It involves treating others with honor and significance. The attitude of kindness is everyday stuff like a great pair of sneakers. Not frilly. Not fancy. Just simple and comfortable.

Humility is next. No matter how much we win or lose in life, God wraps us in a beautiful cloak of grace. When we're humiliated, he loves us exactly as we are. When we're in the limelight, we understand the big part he played in our success.

Meekness is one of my favorite things to wear. Some people think it's nondescript, but I disagree. Meekness makes it possible to endure difficult circumstances and poor treatment at the hands of others. It is a durable garment with interesting textures. And meekness looks different on everyone!

How about *long-suffering?* Sometimes I wish that old rag would just wear out so I could get something more glamorous and colorful. But I know God has fashioned even this to enhance my life. There are times when long-suffering is the only appropriate thing to wear for a particular occasion — and then I'm glad it's in the closet.

Bearing with others and *forgiveness* are the outerwear of God's designs. They are the last things we pull on over everything else before we go out into the world. It would get awfully cold without them. They protect us from the elements and keep the wind from blowing down our necks. As we go in and out of various experiences, we button them up often and keep trudging.

Above all else, Paul says, put on *love.* Without this, we are never fully dressed. You might think of love as your best hat or the jeweled pin on the lapel of life. It is that one essential accessory you should never leave behind. Dust it off, shine it up. Never go out without it!

Put away the shabby clothing of the past and enjoy all the garments in your spiritual wardrobe. Dress like the woman God made you to be. He replaces sackcloth and ashes for garments of praise!

Dear God, thank you for the garments of grace you've prepared for me. I like your style. When I'm feeling poor and ragged, I'll remember you keep your children well dressed. Amen.

Golden Moments

Be strong and do not give up,
for your work will be rewarded.
2 CHRONICLES 15:7

One day I made a list of things I had to do, knowing I was so bewildered and confused by pain that I might forget. I wrote:

1. Get up
2. Survive
3. Go to bed

Some days, this may seem like more work than you'll do the rest of your life. Some days, your work is to be patient with yourself. Other days, your work is just to be yourself.

Recently I met an incredible lady who was so good at the being-patient part. She worked at a large publishing house that produced a huge number of Bibles — all kinds of Bibles in all translations, sizes, and models.

We were shown how the Bibles are assembled, printed, and prepared for packaging and shipment. But one particular step in the process astounded me. You know how we take it for granted that Bibles have those little gold tabs denoting the various books? We came to one station where a woman was sitting on a stool with a pair of tweezers. She was picking up one small gold tab at a time and attaching it to the thin page of the Bible where it belonged.

The amazing thing is that this woman had been doing this for ten years! Over and over again, eight hours a day, four weeks a month, twelve months a year she had been picking up a little gold tab with tweezers and sticking it to a page of a Bible. I thought to myself, *I would last about one Bible doing this, for sure.* And yet I knew that life is made up of routine, and I started thinking about what those things were in my own life: brushing my teeth, making the bed, hanging up my clothes . . .

That day I decided that I wanted to do something to add meaning to all the boring routines in my day. I decided to celebrate them, to make them stand out as worthwhile accomplishments. I started by making a list of the things I do every single day without fail, including weekends. The list started with waking up to the same old alarm buzzer in the morning. It ended with switching off the lamp beside my bed in the evening.

My celebrations began when I traded in my buzzing clock for a radio alarm set to soft music. That was by far the biggest change I made. In other things, I made attitude adjustments. Glancing in the mirror on the way to the bathroom, I started smiling at myself. This started an amazing transformation from the inside out. As I brushed my teeth, I started praising God that I had teeth to brush. Making the bed became a ritual of prayer for my grandchildren. And so on . . .

Each time I faced a tedious, mundane task, I imbued it with enthusiasm. I tried to think up a personally edifying reason for doing what I was doing. I made sure no mundane or trivial task was overlooked. I wanted to fill each one with a sense of being golden, like the stickers placed with care on the pages of those Bibles.

With practice in patience, all my moments are becoming golden. These moments include filling the cat's dish or wiping off countertops, things that take a few seconds or a few minutes. Ho-hum days begin to glow—just enough to make things look rosy. Busy, stressful days are lighter when I remember my resolution to be patient and steady.

Then on really bad days, I think about the patience of the lady sitting on the stool in the publishing house where Bibles are produced by the millions. I think about all the hands that will touch the pages of those Bibles and rely on those little golden tabs. And I believe my tedious moments will be redemptive too.

Oh Lord, because of your life in me, each moment of my life has value and potential for significance—if I will only celebrate it. Infuse my attitude with the fruit of your Spirit, patience. Amen.

Twenty-Five Ways to Make Your Day

I have told you this so that my joy may be in you
and that your joy may be complete.
JOHN 15:11

Give yourself a gift today: Be present with yourself. God is. Enjoy your own personality. God does.

You are going to make it through whatever is on your plate. You are not only a survivor; you are a winner. Here are twenty-five fun, sometimes foolish, always productive ways to put a smile on your face. Make your day!

1. Do the first drudgerous job on your list with a smile. Reward yourself by listening to a great piece of music.
2. Prepare for surprises: Life's most treasured moments come unannounced.
3. Clean and organize one drawer in your house.
4. Write a note to someone you don't know too well just to say, *"Hi, how are you?"*
5. Start a journal if you don't already have one. Write down five things you are thankful for today.
6. Believe you deserve to be happy. Say, "I open my arms wide to the very best God has for me today!"
7. Find something to laugh about today. If all else fails, go get a joke book from the library, call the

funniest person you know, or read this: What do you get when you cross an insomniac, an agnostic, and a dyslexic? Answer: A person who lies awake at night trying to decide if there really is a doG.

8. Do something artsy. Dance to Mozart. Redecorate one wall. Paint a picture. Write a poem.
9. Smile at yourself in the mirror. Wink back.
10. Protect your enthusiasm from the negativity of others. Avoid toxic people today. If you run into one anyway, treat yourself to a double latte.
11. Take a warm loaf of bread to an elderly person or shut-in.
12. Take a power nap.
13. Think about this: If you were going to die tomorrow and were allowed to make only one phone call, who would you call and what would you say? Now, make that call.
14. Remember this: If you cheat on your diet, you gain in the "end."
15. Make eye contact with every person you meet and give a hug to at least half of them.
16. Relish small pleasures.
17. Hold all things loosely and mean it when you say, *"Whatever, Lord!"*
18. Pray for somebody who has offended you.
19. Don't allow a problem to be solved to become more important than a person to be loved.
20. Take the word *struggle* out of your vocabulary and replace it with the word *adventure.*
21. Take one step toward mending a broken relationship.

22. Know this: The present is what slips by us while we're pondering the past and worrying about the future. Live in the now.
23. Remember when you were five years old and just finding out how wonderful you were? Write down the first memory that comes to mind.
24. Ask yourself: What am I doing today that will bring me closer to where I want to be tomorrow?
25. If you don't like your circumstances, find a new way to think about them.

My gracious Father, thank you that you give me a choice every moment about how I feel and respond to life. May I refuse to wait for someone else, but instead make my own day. Amen.

Forgiveness Means Get Over It

Be kind and compassionate to one another,
forgiving each other, just as in Christ God forgave you.
EPHESIANS 4:32

When my third son, Larry, admitted he was a homosexual, I nearly lost my mind. My grief over Larry's behavior was very different from my grief over the deaths of my two older sons, one killed in Vietnam and the other hit by a drunk driver five years later. My grief over Larry was a deep crushing feeling in my chest, a kind of brokenness from which I thought I would never recover. As I've recounted in my book *Stick a Geranium in Your Hat and Be Happy!*, years accumulated under my sorrow, and with those years, I learned to be healthy even in my pain.

When Larry finally did recommit his life to the Lord, we did a radio interview together for Focus on the Family with Dr. James Dobson. On that program, Larry said: "If we as Christians can purpose in our hearts to be kind and loving in all that we do and put away a condemning spirit, and learn the fear of the Lord, then surely the light of Christ will be able to shine in our disbelieving world, and restoration and revival will take root in the lives we touch on a daily basis."

Since that day, these words have been printed on Christmas cards and in church bulletins and shared by audio tape around the world. But before Larry could speak those words, I had to live them out for myself.

There is no way to silence the grief of having to mourn a loved one who has not died. Rage and confusion accompanied the brokenhearted pangs I suffered. I endured the long periods of Larry's absence and rebellion by remembering the good things.

Once when Larry was ten, he was assigned a solo in our church Christmas program. All week at home he'd practice by singing: "While shepherds washed their socks by night all seated on the ground, the angel of the Lord came down and said, 'Will you wash mine?' and said, 'Will you wash mine?'" I told him I'd give him five dollars to sing it like that in the program. (Of course, I was teasing.) He said, *never*. On the night of the program, however, Larry got up and sang it just like he'd practiced, reaping the audience's laughter and applause.

These kinds of memories kept me alive. But guilt had turned me into a recluse. My pain turned to depression. But just as my rope was fraying, I decided to let go of it altogether. I grew so tired of giving Larry to God and taking him back again that I decided to nail my son to the cross. In my imagination I took out a hammer and did just that. I told God, "If Larry never comes home and I never see him again—whatever, Lord!" This is the prayer of relinquishment.

That is when forgiveness took root in my heart. Forgiveness is powerful—not only the ability to forgive, but the ability to be forgiven. I did see Larry again. I asked him to forgive me for the times I hadn't shown understanding or love.

I've seen teenagers wearing T-shirts that say, "Get Over It!" I think Christians should take the lead when it comes to getting over offenses and moving on. Oh, I know, sometimes this is a huge, overwhelming task. But even in long-term grief there is a way to bring closure and to rise above the rage, the guilt, the pain. In Christ this is possible.

Perhaps if the *Guinness Book of World Records* had a section about the world's greatest forgivers, we might see the name of one shining Christian after another. I wonder if Barbara Johnson's name might make it down at the bottom of the list? Would your name be there?

Challenge yourself to stretch farther than you thought you ever could! Take the first step in the long direction of forgiving those who have offended you, hurt you, maimed you for life.

"Get over it"? Perhaps Christians should have thought of this first. Well, maybe they did!

Dear Lord Jesus, we commit ourselves and our loved ones into your hands. We want to be good forgivers — expert forgivers like you are. What we cannot manage to forgive this moment, help us to move toward one degree at a time. Amen.

No Strings Attached

But the fruit of the Spirit is love, joy, peace, patience,
kindness, goodness, faithfulness, gentleness and self-control.
GALATIANS 5:22–23

The little boy had just moved into a new neighborhood.
His name was Brad, and he was very quiet and shy.
One February day when he got home from school he told
his mom he knew Valentine's Day was coming up and he
wanted to make a valentine for every child in his class.

Brad's mom's heart sank. She was certain her little
boy's heart would be hurt in the process of giving,
because every afternoon she watched all the kids walking
home from school, laughing and hanging on to each
other—all except Brad. He trudged along behind them.

But she went along with his idea and bought him
some red and white paper, glue, crayons, and glitter. Day
after day Brad spent his after-school hours painstakingly
creating thirty-five one-of-a-kind valentines.

When the day came to deliver them, he was so
excited. With the precious bundle under his arm, he
raced out the door early to get to school before all his
classmates arrived. His mother thought sadly, *This will
be such a tough day for Brad. I'm going to bake him some of
his favorite cookies and have them warm and ready for him
when he gets home. I wish I could do more to ease the pain
he'll feel when he doesn't get very many valentines.*

That afternoon she put the warm cookies and milk on the table and went to the window to watch for her son. Sure enough, here came the big gang of children, laughing, bright valentines under their arms. And there was Brad, trailing behind. He was walking faster than usual and she thought, *Bless his heart, his arms are empty and he's about to burst into tears.*

When he came into the house she said tenderly, "Honey, Mommy has some warm cookies and milk for you." She was startled to see that his face was aglow. He just marched past her as he declared triumphantly: "I didn't forget a single one . . . not a single one!" He was grinning from ear to ear.

What a message for those of us who forget that the greatest joy is not in receiving, but in giving from our one-of-a-kind hearts. When we get outside ourselves enough to let God's life flow through us, the sweet fruit of his Spirit will grow and nourish everyone around us.

Do you have spiritual fruit in your life today? What are you doing to actively show love and kindness to other people in the humble spirit of Christ? If you have been caught up in what you are — or are not — getting from others, think about little Brad. Then ask God how he wants to use your one-of-a-kind self to touch someone today. Give his love away with joy in your heart. No strings attached.

Lord Jesus, remind me continually that your love seeks nothing for itself but gives generously out of its abundance. Because you love me, I always have enough love to give away to anyone who crosses my path. Let me experience the joy of giving in your name. Amen.

Be a Joy Germ

Like cold water to a weary soul is good news
from a distant land.
PROVERBS 25:25

In my college there was a sweet tradition: Each evening about nine o'clock a young man would bring notes from guys to the girls' dormitory. A bell would ring, and we girls would dash down to the lobby. The notes usually asked for a date or to sit with a favorite girl at a performance, or contained just a few affectionate words.

For some girls, this was a painful tradition because there were never notes for them. I remember one girl who was just a little "different." Her clothes never matched or fit right and she had difficulty speaking clearly. She stopped coming down or expecting anything. Then one night her name was called out. It happened several nights in a row, then at least once or twice a week. Each time she received an anonymous note complimenting her on some special thing she did that was appreciated. The notes were like a gift straight from God to her.

This girl never did find out who sent her the notes, but the fellow who had written them became a good friend of mine and confided in me about it. He was sort of "different," too. He'd lost his hair due to a childhood disease and also had a speech impediment. But he had a gentle and sensitive spirit. He cared enough to let one individual know how special she was beyond what people saw on the outside. He changed her picture of herself that year.

When we do little acts of kindness that make life more bearable for someone else, we are walking in love as the Bible commands us. One way to do this costs only the sum of a postage stamp, a little paper, and ink. Every one of us has felt the nudge to write someone a letter or note. Many times we don't follow up on it; we tell ourselves it wouldn't matter anyway. When we think this way, we miss giving and receiving splashes of joy.

I receive many notes from women who are hurting or burdened, yet care enough to let me know my ministry has meant something to them. I put their notes in my joy box, and when I need a special pick-me-up I sit down and read them all over again. Sometimes the salutation alone means as much as the message itself. Sometimes the beauty of the card inspires me. Or the handwriting is full of emotion, or there are cute stickers that make me smile.

Someone you know is crossing a desert in her life and can use a drink of cold water. Will you be the one to bring it to her? Take up your pen! In the deserts of life, hearts shrivel up. We can't let others dehydrate from neglect.

Why not clear out a drawer in your kitchen and fill it with stationery, pens, and fun stickers? In between clean-up jobs or while you're watching the potatoes bake, you can jot a little love letter to someone. Get your kids into the act! Teach them early to think of others' needs and reach out in a tangible way. A few words is all it takes. If you know someone is going through a long-term sorrow, pre-address and stamp some envelopes so it's easy to jot a thought and drop it in the mailbox once or twice a month.

Be a joy germ and find your own unique way to share a word of encouragement today. Someone you know needs it!

Dear Lord, we need encouragement, and we need to give it too. Take our minds and pens and time and use them to uplift someone else, for your glory. Amen.

Enjoy the Ride!

For a thousand years in thy sight are but as yesterday
when it is past, and as a watch in the night.
PSALM 90:4 KJV

Yesterday is a sacred room in your heart where you
keep your memories. Here you cherish laughter from
another day. You hear melodies of half-forgotten songs.
You feel the warmth of a hug from an old friend. You see
the lingering glow of a long-gone love. From your yesterdays you draw lessons and encouragement to pass
along to others.

My heart smiled at some yesterdays recently when I
thought back on teaching my oldest son, Tim, how to
drive. We practiced in a nearby cemetery where it was
quiet, the posted speed limits were very slow, and traffic
was sparse. *A nice, safe place to start,* I thought.

Tim would work his way around the curves and turns,
carefully maneuvering the car through its paces. Brake
into the curve. Gently. Accelerate out of the curve.
Slowly. Smoothly. Stop. Reverse. Back up. Park between
the lines. Try it again. Start all over again.

Afterward, we'd go over to In-N-Out Hamburgers
across the street where I would recover from the experience. After we ate, Tim would want to tackle the curves
again. Sometimes I wondered if I would survive until he
actually learned to drive.

Well, I did. Tim did learn. And he was a good driver. But years later, his car was smashed by someone who wasn't. Now, Tim's grave is right up there where he practiced driving.

I can be bitter about it. Or I can be better. When yesterdays bring bittersweet memories, I can fume and blame my losses on someone else, or I can let my memories comfort me and provide encouragement to someone else.

As I was standing by Tim's grave recently and thinking of the many times we wound around those curving lanes, I remembered how I used to feel—nervous and tense but trying not to show it. My reverie by Tim's headstone was interrupted when a little red Nissan came around the curve. There was a mother, about thirty-five, her hair blowing in the breeze. Beside her, in the driver's seat, sat a boy, about fifteen, cute as anything. The mom's face looked intent while the boy tried to look nonchalant.

I wanted to shout out, "Enjoy the ride! Now! Make a memory of your experience. Go get a hamburger to celebrate. Do it now, while you still can look each other in the eyes!"

Yes, it hurts. I wish Tim were here, driving me to some of the places I need to go occasionally, just for old times' sake. I long for the family circle—unbroken—the way it will be in heaven. I want to hear my boy's laughter again and the way he used to rush in the house and call, "Mom!" I envy that mom in the little red Nissan, but I know the years end up stealing something from everybody. And I just want to tell that woman to savor the moment. Taste the present full strength. Do everything you can to hold it close.

This week when I go do the things I have to do, I'll take my own advice. I'll look people in the eyes, and if they don't have a smile, I'll give them one of mine. I'll make a date with my husband or play a joke on a friend. I won't let time pass without reminding myself, "Enjoy the ride!"

Dear God, I'm ready for adventure. Let's make a memory! Amen.

The God Who Sees

She gave this name to the LORD who spoke to her:
"You are the God who sees me."
GENESIS 16:13

Hagar, the pregnant maidservant of Sarah, had fled into the wilderness. She just wanted to die. But God sent an angel who found her and told her to go back home even though it was the hardest place to go. He then predicted that the child born to her would be a wild man who wouldn't get along with anybody.

Now I don't know about you, but if I were Hagar, that's not exactly what I would have wanted to hear. Hagar's response, however, was to call God a name that had never been used before: *The-God-Who-Sees*. And she accepted what he said.

Yes, our God is the all-knowing One who sees our scars, our secrets, and our strength. Our wounds and shame are his affair, and he knows just how much trouble we can stand. Somehow, the fact that he knows us so well makes a difference. We understand there is a direction and we are part of a bigger picture. From the wildernesses in our lives, the fact that *he sees* gives us a reason to carry on. No longer are we anonymous, lonely, and lost.

I wonder what kind of reception Hagar got when she returned to the campsite of Sarah and Abraham? The Bible doesn't tell us. But five chapters and fourteen years later, the Lord visited Sarah. Her life, also, had been burdened and full of trouble. The root of her problem was not fertility, like Hagar's, but infertility.

Once, years before, Sarah had laughed sarcastically at messengers who predicted she would have a baby. It seemed a ridiculous thing since she was long past childbearing age. When confronted with the fact that she'd laughed behind closed doors, Sarah denied it (Gen. 18:10–15). But that didn't change the facts. God knew. He is The-God-Who-Sees our secrets. In spite of what we try to hide from him, he leads us toward our destiny.

At a ripe old age, Sarah bore a boy named Isaac and laughed again. But this time the sarcasm was gone. This time, it was just fun, hilarity, and real toe-tingling joy. She said right out loud: "God has made me laugh." But the part I like best is when Sarah added, "and everyone who hears about this will laugh with me" (Gen. 21:6). I think God has given women the power to move on in life through the contagion of laughter.

I've spent the past several years collecting quips about laughter and sayings that make me laugh. I have a lot of quotes about dieting, middle age, motherhood, husbands, wrinkles, love — you name it: all those hot spots in a woman's life that would kill us if we let them get us down. The secret is to *not* let them get you down. The secret of not letting them get you down is to laugh about them. In fact, I try to find ways to make the saddest things funny.

We can sigh about things, or we can laugh. Both these responses release pressure, but which is the most fun? We laugh so we won't scream. Laughter is a riotous vote of acceptance that he is *The-God-Who-Sees*. Whatever it is probably won't go away, so we might as well live and laugh through it. When we double over laughing, we're bending so we won't break. If you think your particular troubles are too heavy and too traumatic to laugh about, remember that laughing is like changing a baby's diaper. It doesn't solve any problems permanently, but it makes things more acceptable for a while.

You have a choice. Laugh in sarcasm or laugh with joy. Try it both ways, then write and tell me what worked for you!

Dear Jesus, teach me to laugh, but don't let me forget I cried. Amen.

A Gift from the Scrap Pile

So take a new grip with your tired hands, stand firm on your
shaky legs, and mark out a straight, smooth path for your
feet so that those who follow you, though weak and lame,
will not fall and hurt themselves, but become strong.

HEBREWS 12:12–13 TLB

Charles Darrow was out of work and as poor as a pauper
during the Depression, but he kept a smile on his face
and a sparkle in his eye. He didn't want his wife, expecting their first child, to be discouraged; so every night when
he returned to their little apartment after standing in the
unemployment lines all day, he would tell her funny stories about the things he had seen—or imagined.

Darrow was a clever man, and he was always coming
up with notions that made people laugh. (He wasn't at all
like the lady who said she once had a bright idea—but it
died of loneliness.)

Darrow knew how powerfully his own attitude
affected his wife. His temperament was the color his wife
used to paint her own mood. If he came home weary and
irritable, her spirits fell, and her smile vanished. On the
other hand, if she heard him whistling a merry tune as he
climbed the many flights of stairs up to their tiny rooms,
she would fling open the door and scamper out to the
railing to lean over and smile at him as he wound his way
up the staircase. They fed on the gift of each other's joy.

In his younger years, Darrow had enjoyed happy family vacations in nearby Atlantic City, and he drew on those memories to keep his spirits high. He developed a little game on a square piece of cardboard. Around the edges he drew a series of "properties" named after the streets and familiar places he had visited during those pleasant childhood summers. He carved little houses and hotels out of scraps of wood, and as he and his young wife played the game each evening, they pretended to be rich, buying and selling property and "building" homes and hotels like extravagant tycoons. On those long, dark evenings, that impoverished apartment was filled with the sound of laughter.

Charles Darrow didn't set out to become a millionaire when he developed Monopoly, the game that was later marketed around the world by Parker Brothers, but that's what happened. The little gift he developed from scraps of cardboard and tiny pieces of wood was simply a way to keep his wife's spirits up during her Depression-era pregnancy; ultimately, that gift came back to him as bountiful riches.

Monopoly is still being sold by the thousands more than fifty years later. Every time I think of those little green houses and red hotels, the unusual game pieces, and those "get out of jail" cards that made us all race around the game board with gleeful abandon, I see an example of shared joy. Darrow created a gift of joy, shared it with the world, and the gift came right back to him a thousandfold.

Are times tough in your little apartment—or lavish mansion? Are you weary from standing in lines that lead to nowhere? If it seems as if your world is collapsing around you and you feel yourself slipping down into the depths of depression, don't despair. As someone said,

"Even the sun sinks every night—but it rises again every morning." Remember that the right temperature in a home is maintained by warm hearts, not by icy glares, lukewarm enthusiasm—or hotheads! Your attitude can set the tone for your whole family. So use whatever scraps you can find—even if, in the beginning, it's just a scrap of a smile—and make a gift of whatever you have. Then watch the gifts come back to you.

Dear Lord, when times are tough, please help me see that your gifts of love and grace are always there for me. Show me how I can pull together the scraps of my life, tie them up with your love, and share that gift with others. Amen.

Dot-to-Dot Living

"For I know the plans I have for you," declares the LORD,
"plans to prosper you and not to harm you,
plans to give you hope and a future."
JEREMIAH 29:11

My darling daughter-in-love, Shannon, says life is like a dot-to-dot picture. When you begin, you have no idea what your life is going to turn out to be. You start at one dot, and then another dot appears, and, hoping for the best, you jump off the first dot to land on the next one.

Sometimes a dot can be a huge, black hole. And other times, the dot is empty, like a zero with the rim rubbed out. Occasionally, dots are tear shaped. On others you feel like dancing—maybe those are the polka dots!

You have to be well along in life before the big picture becomes apparent. Even then, just when you think you have it figured out, the next dot can pull you way off to the edge—or even over the edge—and then you realize this isn't the picture you thought it was. Not at all.

Sometimes the dots are arranged in a twisted way that makes no sense, and you wonder where on earth this life is taking you. You think maybe you're lost. You imagine that there is no big picture, that you're trudging along on this stupid dot trail, and you're never going to get back to the source so the picture can be completed.

Some dots have different shapes; some are stretched into a smile, and others have the form of a heart. How you love those dots! But they're hard to leave, those little lighthearted dots, and you find yourself clinging to them, unwilling to let go, until suddenly they vanish from underneath your feet, and you flail and grope pitifully through the nothingness left beneath you until finally you gain another foothold.

Sometimes you're afraid to step off a dot that's become comfortable and familiar. You look out across the wide expanse of challenges, and you wonder if you'll even make it to the next dot. It takes courage to leap across the vast unknown to land on a strange and foreign dot.

Then there comes a big, black dot that is all-encompassing in its darkness. In fact, it's not a dot at all but a vast sea of black that stretches endlessly in all directions. Sinking into the gloom, you realize there's no way out. You struggle and fight, but there's only more darkness. Finally you give up, unable to struggle through the inky pit of despair one more moment.

It is at that point, says Shannon, that another dot appears. In the vast universe of blackness, it is white—a tiny, glowing pinpoint of light. The light is God, and the beam it casts is his rope of rescue. You wrap its warmth around you, cling to it, and feel yourself rising out of the blackness.

Then, standing beside God in all his glory, at last you can see the picture, a line that continues from dot to dot, forming a life. "Oh, Father!" you cry, turning to thank him for this moment of clarity. It is then that you see what he holds in his hand—an artist's paintbrush. And on its fine-tipped bristles clings a tiny dot of ink.

Dear Father, you already know every moment of my life, from beginning to end. Thank you for being a lamp for my feet and a light for my path. Amen.

Bountiful Blessings

Do not repay evil with evil or insult with insult,
but with blessing, because to this you were called
so that you may inherit a blessing.
1 PETER 3:9

A man named Sebastian decided to masquerade as a priest to please his dying Aunt Esther, whose fortune he wanted to inherit. She had always hoped he would become a clergyman.

It was all just an act. Sebastian was far from being a godly man. In fact, he was one of those characters people describe as worthless unless sold by the pound. But a strange thing happened whenever he wore his clerical costume. He found himself becoming nicer to others. He left bigger tips in restaurants, even when the food was bad. He was more patient while driving in rush-hour traffic. And people were unexpectedly nice to him in return.

Sebastian, not a Christian at that point, had probably never read God's promise in Proverbs 11:25, "He who refreshes others will himself be refreshed." So Sebastian was surprised by what happened to him. He was so moved by his experiences that eventually he became a real priest. He had discovered the truth in the saying, "Love, like paint, can make things beautiful when you spread it, but it simply dries up when you don't use it."

Sebastian no longer wore a costume; he was clad in the "garment of praise instead of a spirit of despair" (Isa. 61:3).

Actually, Sebastian is a character in Alfred Alcorn's novel, *Vestments*. Unlike Sebastian, I've found that as God showers me with blessings and as I share them with others, I've received so much love in return that I'm no longer surprised. The rebounding "surprises" have become delightfully dependable.

For example, the people whose lives are touched by Spatula Ministries, the organization Bill and I operate to help parents who are dealing with the death or alienation of their children, often respond by asking how they can help someone else—a perfect example of rebounding blessings. That happened recently when a distraught mother called me from a trailer park in the Northwest. She was going through a very painful time, and she had heard I was coming to a nearby city for a women's seminar.

"Barb, I don't have the money to buy a ticket, but it would help me so much if I could just talk with you a minute," she said. "I know it's a lot to ask, but could you meet me outside the auditorium when you have a spare minute? I'd wait all day if I thought I'd get to see you! And I'd bring my copies of your books for you to sign."

Promising to call her back when the weekend's schedule was finalized, I hung up the phone, my heart aching for the anguished mother. Then, just a few days later, a letter came from another mom in the Northwest who had finally emerged from the tunnel of an especially painful ordeal that had nearly destroyed her life.

She was grateful for all that her new Spatula friends had done for her, and she said she wanted to pass along the blessing that had been shared with her. "What can I do, Barb?" she asked. "How can I help?"

Looking at her letter, something tugged at me, something about her return address. The woman lived in a trailer park, and its name rang a bell in my memory. In a flash I was on the phone to her. "There's a woman who lives in your trailer park, and she could use some encouragement right now."

"I'm on my way," the other mother said excitedly.

Not only did she reach out to the woman who had called me, but she also gave that woman enough money to buy tickets to the seminar, not just for herself but for several friends as well. As a result, all of us received a special splash of joy that day as we realized how God had reached out to two far-apart corners of our country and brought us all together to refresh each other and share each other's burdens — and blessings.

Ardath Rodale, CEO of Rodale Press, said, "Inhale all the good that surrounds you, and as you exhale, give it away by sharing with others." As you breathe this way, no doubt you'll discover another sage's wise observation: "One of the most beautiful compensations of life is that no one can sincerely try to help another without helping herself."

Dear God, thank you for all the joyful blessings you have splashed upon my life. Please help me be creative in finding ways I can share those blessings with others. Amen.

The Most Powerful Perfume

> But thanks be to God, who . . . through us spreads
> everywhere the fragrance of the knowledge of him.
>
> 2 CORINTHIANS 2:14

"Aromatherapy" is a recent trend that teaches certain aromas can have powerful effects on our psyches. Commercials selling these aromas usually feature a woman relaxing in a bubble bath with her eyes closed and her head leaned back on a pillow. A peaceful smile graces the woman's face, which seems to float serenely on the cloud of bubbles billowing up under her chin. Just one whiff of this special fragrance, the ads seem to say, and you're twenty years younger, thirty pounds thinner, and forty times more likely to have Ed McMahon ring your doorbell and announce you've just won fifty million dollars.

In my case, any scents, therapeutic or not, detour through the kitchen before they reach my psyche. The truth is I have a hard time smelling anything—from flowers (which remind me of picnics in the park) to smoke (the signal in our home that dinner is done)—without having some image of food popping into my head. The pleasure I receive from thinking about food is second only to actually eating it. Just visualizing a hot fudge sundae or a succulent prime rib can send me drifting off to mindless bliss—and to the nearest restaurant! (As Bill says, "Barb cooks for fun, but for food, we go out!")

But all this "scent sense" is nothing new. Long ago, when I was in college, I waited tables in the campus dining room, which served big, fluffy, yeast-raised dinner rolls for Sunday dinner. Sitting in church on Sunday mornings, the aroma of those tantalizing dinner rolls would waft through the chapel windows, beckoning me to work (and to eat; we kitchen workers always sneaked a little "preview roll," just to make sure they were up to par). Like a shepherd's crook, the fragrance of that warm, flaky bread reached into the church pew every Sunday and pulled me out, toward the source of that wonderful smell.

"'Scuse me, 'scuse me," I would whisper as I scooted to the end of the pew and out the door. "I have to go to work."

Yes, indirectly at least, I'm as vulnerable to aromatherapy as anyone else—and have been for a long time. And there's one place where aromatherapy is really powerful, for me at least. I never really understood why until I read David Koenig's book *Mouse Tales* (Bonaventure Press, 1994), which shares some behind-the-scenes secrets about Disneyland, just a twenty-minute drive from our home in Southern California. It turns out Walt Disney and his "imagineers" recognized the connection between scent and psyche long before the current aromatherapists made their discovery.

Whenever I walk down Main Street in Disneyland, I find myself smiling at everyone, even at that rambunctious family of twelve who cut me off at the entrance turnstiles a few minutes earlier. Before I know it, my mood has changed from harried tourist ready to rip the tires off the next baby stroller that runs over my toes to gracious guest sauntering jovially down the sidewalk on the verge of whistling "Zippity-Doo-Dah."

Part of the magical mood change comes from the subtle waves of scent that waft over the make-believe marketplace. From hidden vents in front of the Candy Palace comes the soothing scent of vanilla. At Christmastime, it's peppermint. And, I'm told, a couple of thousand miles away in Hershey, Pennsylvania, the same thing—only in wafts of chocolate—greets visitors to Chocolate World.

Fragrance can indeed be a powerful but invisible force, influencing more than just our taste buds. With the irresistible power of a tidal wave, it can sweep over us, changing what had seemed unchangeable: our attitudes.

God's Word is like that too. It works its invisible power over us in ways that can be subtle or overwhelming. As C. S. Lewis said, it "whispers to us in our joys, speaks to us in our difficulties, and shouts to us in our pain." It changes our moods, reworks our attitudes, and infuses us with courage. We inhale God's love and exhale his goodness, breathe in his grace, and breathe out his praise.

Like the woman in the bathtub, we soak ourselves in God's love, and it bubbles up around us, lifting our chins, soothing our spirits, easing our troubles, and bringing us peace in the midst of pain. It's the most effective therapy in the universe, and its fragrance clings to us wherever we go. We hope that others, passing through our lives, catch a whiff of God's love and find their attitudes changing and their hearts yearning for the Source.

Gracious Lord, infuse me with the fragrance of your Word so that others sense in me the depth of your love and the joy of your presence. Amen.

Encouraging Words

Anxious hearts are very heavy
but a word of encouragement does wonders!
PROVERBS 12:25 TLB

On that stormy night when the disciples saw Jesus walking on the water, they were scared out of their wits, thinking he was a ghost. But Jesus told them quietly, "Don't be afraid."

Peter, always the outspoken one, answered first. "Lord, if it's really you, tell me to come to you on the water." And Jesus simply replied, "Come."

If you're a parent, you can probably remember when your children were first learning to walk. As they stood there, wobbling unsteadily, you probably said to them, ever so gently, "Come on. You can do it. Come on. Just try. Take a step."

Our arms outstretched, we coaxed and encouraged them. Eventually, believing our faith in them, they let go of the coffee table or Daddy's pant leg or the bathtub, and they took that first awesome step.

What wonders a bit of encouragement can do! It's one of the most awesome treasures God has given us — the ability to inspire, motivate, and reassure others.

Even babies have it. Scientists say a natural progression of infants' development is to learn to clap their hands together. That must mean God has given them a way to cheer on us parents (and God knows we need all the encouragement we can get!).

The apostle Paul reminded all of us, young and old alike, that if we've been given the gift of encouragement—and who of us hasn't at some time in our lives?—then we're to use it! (See Rom. 12:8.)

Encouragement doesn't have to be profound. After all, Jesus encouraged the skeptical Peter to do the impossible with one little word: "Come." It just needs to be expressed.

Someone once said that encouragement is simply reminding a person of the "shoulders" he's standing on, the heritage he's been given. That's what happened when a young man, the son of a star baseball player, was drafted by one of the minor league teams. As hard as he tried, his first season was disappointing, and by mid-season he expected to be released any day.

The coaches were bewildered by his failure because he possessed all the characteristics of a superb athlete, but he couldn't seem to incorporate those advantages into a coordinated effort. He seemed to have become disconnected from his potential.

His future seemed darkest one day when he had already struck out his first time at bat. Then he stepped up to the batter's box again and quickly ran up two strikes. The catcher called a time-out and trotted to the pitcher's mound for a conference. While they were busy, the umpire, standing behind the plate, spoke casually to the boy.

Then play resumed, the next pitch was thrown—and the young man knocked it out of the park. That was the turning point. From then on, he played the game with a new confidence and power that quickly drew the attention of the parent team, and he was called up to the majors.

On the day he was leaving for the city, one of his coaches asked him what had caused such a turnaround. The young man replied it was the encouraging remark the umpire had made that day when his baseball career had seemed doomed.

"He told me I reminded him of all the times he had stood behind my dad in the batter's box," the boy explained. "He said I was holding the bat just the way Dad had held it. And he told me, 'I can see his genes in you; you have your father's arms.' After that, whenever I swung the bat, I just imagined I was using Dad's arms instead of my own."

Like that young baseball player, we all have our heavenly Father's "genes." But sometimes we need to be reminded of the great potential we possess. We need someone to point out our likeness to the One who created us, to see God's image in us.

Just one little word of encouragement can make all the difference. Soon we're ready to step back up to the plate and take a swing at whatever life throws at us.

Dear Lord, please give me the right words of encouragement to lift someone's heart today. Amen.

Drunk Without Drinking

Dear friends, since God so loved us,
we also ought to love one another.
1 JOHN 4:11

When I was preparing to undergo some minor surgery recently, the doctor warned me that the anesthesia might make me a little goofy even hours after the surgery was completed. For a moment I wondered whether anyone who knew me and thought I was already pretty goofy would even notice. Then I remembered that it's my husband, Bill, who's the peculiar one, being an only child and all.

The doctor said that, when I left the hospital, I was not to drive a car, sign any contracts, or make any irrevocable decisions because I would be considered legally drunk for twenty-four hours after the surgery. Never having had a drink of alcohol in my life, I had no idea what to expect. *Just think,* I told myself, *you're gonna be drunk without even taking a drink!*

The idea was so amazing to me that I started imagining I was drunk even before the surgery started. When I arrived at the outpatient desk, the receptionist shoved a stack of papers toward me and told me to "fill them out, check the things that apply, and then sign here, here, and here. Be sure to press hard, because it's a triplicate form."

In my imaginary state of drunkenness, I had a little trouble following her rapid-fire instructions, but I finally completed them all. In just a moment the door opened, and a nurse called me in. As soon as she had me settled in a bed, three other nurses slipped through the curtain.

"Oh, Mrs. Johnson," one of them said in a low, excited voice, "we're so thrilled to have you here. When we saw your name on the admittance forms and realized it was you, we called you back early. All of us have read your books. I even have one of them here, and I was hoping you would sign it for me."

I wanted to beg off, pleading imaginary drunkenness, but since she was a nurse she would know I hadn't had any anesthesia yet. So I signed her book and then looked at the four of them expectantly, wondering what would happen next.

They stood around my bed, their faces glowing with friendly smiles. Suddenly my little cubicle had taken on a party atmosphere. I wondered if it was because I was drunk — and then I remembered I wasn't, at least not yet.

"Barb, could we pray with you before your surgery?" one of the nurses said.

Enthusiastically, the four of them joined hands, and the two nearest me clasped my hands in their own, and they prayed the sweetest prayer I'd ever heard. (Of course I thought I was inebriated, so just about everything was sounding pretty good to me then!)

Outside the curtain, I heard a man clear his throat. "Oh, Dr. Brown!" one of the nurses said, peeking out of the curtain. "We're just saying a little prayer for Barb. Would you mind waiting a minute?"

Evidently he agreed, because she returned and the prayer continued.

In just a moment the nurses' prayers ended, and the anesthesiologist stepped up to my bed and gave me a reassuring pat on the arm. He too said a little prayer, asking

God to be with all of us in that operating room. Under ordinary circumstances I might have become a little apprehensive, knowing the moment had come for the surgery to commence. But he held my hand, and in my imaginary drunkenness—and having just heard the nurses pray for me so thoughtfully and sincerely—I managed to flash him a smile before the lights went out . . .

To be honest, I don't think I was ever "drunk" during those twenty-four hours after my surgery, but I certainly was on a high. I kept remembering those thoughtful nurses and how they had surrounded me with their love and held my hands in theirs—and then sent me off to La-La Land with their prayers echoing through my mind and filling my heart with peace. The joy that memory brought me erased any discomfort the minor surgery might have caused.

By that evening, I was feeling fine—and even a little mischievous. Knowing Bill had been warned by the doctor to beware of my expected intoxication, I could tell he was constantly watching me out of the corner of his eye. For just a moment, I was tempted to put a lampshade on my head and dance a jig on the sidewalk, and then call up a real estate agent and sell the house. But just imagining how startled Bill would be was enough fun. And besides, being peculiar is his job.

Dear Father, we are so grateful to you for sending your representatives into our lives to hold our hands and pray for us when fear threatens our peace. Your love is intoxicating, Lord! It heals us, sustains us, and fills our lives with joy. Thank you! Amen.

Little Reminders

Let your light shine before men, that they may see your
good deeds and praise your Father in heaven.
MATTHEW 5:16

Unable to find what I needed in a store recently, I sought out a salesperson for assistance. Finally I found one of the red-vested clerks, but he was bent over a large box, focused on a search of his own.

Seeing his resolute face and hurried manner, I hesitated to interrupt him. Then I spotted the name tag bouncing around on the shoulder of his vest. It bore a smiley face.

And below his name, Caleb, was this statement: "Ask me! I like to help."

Encouraged by that suggestion, I cleared my throat and said, "Excuse me, please. Could you help me?"

Caleb jerked his head out of the box and then straightened up when he saw me. Suddenly his seriousness was transformed into a warm smile. "Yes, ma'am! What can I do for you?" That smiley face and the message on Caleb's name tag had reassured me that I could expect a kind response from him. The incident reminded me of the messages and symbols we Christians wear to tell others who we are. (It's also a little like we senior citizens who wear name tags to our fiftieth high school reunions — to remind ourselves who we are!) How reassuring it is to see one of those little symbols when we need to approach a stranger to ask for help or to make some other request.

My son Barney knows all about that. A few years ago, when he owned a concrete business, a mishap occurred on one of his residential jobs. He was pouring concrete around someone's swimming pool when one of the side panels of the form collapsed and some of the concrete oozed onto a neighbor's property. By the time he got the mixer turned off and the chute closed up, there was an awful calamity!

He dreaded telling the neighbor what had happened. He imagined the person ranting, raving, threatening lawsuits, and all sorts of grievances when he or she saw the problem Barney's accident had created. So when Barney walked up the neighbor's driveway, his heart was pounding and his palms were sweating.

Then, as he walked by the neighbor's car, he saw something that eased his worries. There, just above the back bumper, was a simple decal—two curved lines that started at a point and ended by crossing over each other. A little fish.

Encouraged by that wordless promise, Barney rang the doorbell. When the woman answered the door, he showed her the problem, apologized for the mess, and promised to restore everything fully and pay for any other damages the escaping concrete might have caused. The woman listened in silence to all that Barney had to say. Then he ended up with, "I was really apprehensive about coming and telling you this, but then I saw the little fish on your car, and I thought, *Thank you, Lord! She's a Christian! She'll understand—and she'll forgive me.*"

And sure enough, the woman did. (After all, what else could she do once Barney had pointed out the symbol she'd stuck on her car for all to see?) She graciously accepted Barney's apology and even invited him inside for a glass of ice water. It takes courage to wear the symbols of Christianity. As soon as you slap a fish-shaped decal on your car, some turkey shows up at your door saying he's just dumped a load of concrete all over your patio. While you're reading that Christian magazine in the checkout line, the two-year-old behind you is swiping your white, wool skirt with a dripping chocolate ice-cream cone. As soon as you pin that little cross to your lapel, one of your kids walks in the door and asks you to tell a little white lie—just this once—to get him out of big trouble at school.

It's much easier to wear a Christian symbol under your coat or carry it in your purse—or hide it under a bushel. It takes real courage to hang it out there for all the world to see. Whether you wear a tiny, fish-shaped lapel pin or paint "Truckin' for Jesus" in letters two feet high on the side of your eighteen-wheeler, it's all the same to those who are watching. For some of them, the only Jesus they've ever known is the Jesus they see in you.

Gracious Father, please fill me with your light so my shortcomings are overshadowed and your goodness shines through. Amen.

Delightfully Deceived

> Do not forget to entertain strangers, for by so doing some
> people have entertained angels without knowing it.
> HEBREWS 13:2

Our youngest son, Barney, was planning a surprise
party for his wife, Shannon, at a hotel in San Diego,
and he invited Bill and me to join the fun. On a lark, we
decided to take the train, and we invited my friend Lynda
along.

After our train arrived, we jostled our carry-on bags
into the train station, expecting Barney to be waiting for
us on the platform. All the other passengers scurried
around as we stood there, scanning the crowd for Barney's handsome face. But he wasn't there.

We shuffled our things over to a bench to wait. Grad-
ually, the large waiting area emptied, and we were alone.
I dug through my purse for a quarter and the number of
the hotel where we were supposed to stay. The only pay
phone in sight was way off in the corner, and as Lynda
and I walked toward it, a disheveled man leaning against
the wall raised his head and watched us.

From beneath a tattered baseball cap, his long, scraggly, black hair fell over his eyes and hung in tangles. His
stained and wrinkled trousers were four sizes too big.
One part of his ragged shirttail hung outside his sagging
waistband while the rest was loosely stuffed inside. His

canvas shoes were as holey as Swiss cheese. Little clouds of smoke rose out of the cigarette that dangled from his mouth.

My heart lurched a little at the unexpected sight, and Lynda must have been startled by the man's appearance as well, because she reached for my arm and said, "Barb . . ." as she made a frightened face.

"Just imagine," I told her, patting her hand reassuringly, "that poor man is someone's kid."

I made the call, only to find Barney wasn't at the hotel. "I guess we'll just have to wait. He probably got stopped for another traffic ticket."

As soon as I sat on the bench, the disheveled man slowly ambled toward us.

"Barb, he's coming toward us!" Lynda gasped, scooting closer to me on the bench.

"No, he's not," I hissed back, turning my head and pretending to look the other way while noting his every move out of the corner of my eye.

"He is! He's gonna rob us!" Lynda's lips didn't move, but her words were distinct.

The man's hands were in his pockets, and he was staring at us as he drew nearer.

I began to shuffle through my purse, trying to decide whether to offer him a couple of dollars—or a breath mint. Bill, engrossed in a magazine, was oblivious to the unfolding drama. I elbowed him, causing him to turn to me impatiently. "What?" he said too loudly.

The man was now less than ten feet away from us, and my heart was pounding. Lynda squirmed next to me on the bench, and the three of us sat there huddled together, watching the ragged man come nearer. Suddenly he spoke.

"Hi, Mom!"

Mom? If I wore dentures, they would have clattered to the floor. I stared at the man, who stood so close to me now I could look up under the bill of the baseball cap and peer into those twinkling dark eyes, those suddenly familiar eyes . . .

"Barney, it's you! What on earth . . . ?"

Now he was laughing so hard he couldn't talk. Wordlessly, he lifted off the cap — and the long, scraggly, black hair came off with it, a wig attached to the cap. The cigarette was fake too; it emitted clouds of powder rather than smoke whenever Barney puffed on it. With a smile as wide as the Mississippi, he hitched up his enormous trousers while pulling me into his arms for a hug. Still feeling a little bewildered, I suddenly regretted all those tricks I had played on my family during our boys' growing-up years. Now, I realized, it was payback time.

Since that moment, I have developed a new empathy for how poor old Isaac must have felt when his conniving son Jacob showed up at Isaac's bedside disguised as his older brother, Esau. And I have a new understanding of the Scripture passage that says, "Can a mother forget her little child and not have love for her own son? Yet even if that should be, I will not forget you" (Isa. 49:15 TLB).

Even when we're so low down and hard up our own mothers wouldn't recognize us, God sees through our disguises. He looks into our hearts and calls us his own.

Dear Lord, you have promised not to forget me, even when I foolishly disguise myself in the ways of the world. Thank you for always remembering me and welcoming me back into your everlasting arms. Amen.

The Whole World in His Hands

May the favor of the Lord our God rest upon us;
establish the work of our hands for us—
yes, establish the work of our hands.

Psalm 90:17

Do you remember when every house had a clothes-line and the "hand work" that went into washing those fresh-air-scented linens? How about the toasty feel of a wood fire burning first thing in the morning? In those days the ingredients for a good meal were grown in a garden and simmered for flavor all day.

Would you trade a modern convenience or two for one of those old-fashioned "luxuries"? Or would they all be too much trouble, taking too much time?

Something about handmade things brings serenity. They represent more than tedious hours or backbreaking work. I think they are to our souls what water is to a fish—the context in which to thrive. The soul thrives, as Ralph Waldo Emerson said, on "a little fire, a little food, and an immense quiet."

Would Martha Stewart agree? I'm not certain she's into the soul of things, but she's a woman who knows how to use her hands!

The problem is, when I try to copy Martha's style, I end up with one nerve left . . . and someone is bound to get on it! Wanting a Currier and Ives holiday, I end up with *As the World Turns*. I believe if you show me a woman whose home is always ready for company, I'll show you a woman who is too tired to entertain.

I want the handmade life but fall far short of soulful serenity. How to make both work? While Martha Stewart excels in the work of her hands, I ask myself, *What would Jesus do with his hands to bring graciousness and love to this world?*

Jesus would express welcome in a handshake and offer unconditional love in a hug. He would sit and listen, holding somebody else's hands folded in his own. He would wrestle fishing nets from the sea, tickle a kid, carve a beautiful piece of wooden furniture. I bet he knew how to paint, put a house together, build an altar, plant a garden, and give a back rub. If this kind of handmade love is freely given in a home, Jesus' presence will be felt there.

Use your hands to express humor, articulate a joke, elaborate a funny story. I used my hands for fun times when I was raising my four boys. From Jell-O fights to backyard baseball games, humor reminds children that adults can let down their guard. We don't always have to take ourselves so seriously.

Use hands to embrace precious moments too. Caress a baby's cheek, stroke an arm, dry a tear. Spread hope in a hand around a shoulder, pick up someone who has fallen down, give the thumbs-up sign.

God gave us hands to give and to receive his blessings. Think of all the intricate and amazing things you do with your hands all day long: The way your fingers work together kneading bread or work separately to type a note. Your thumbs can grip a heavy object or stroke a kitten. The palm of your hand can rub a kink out of someone's back or smooth a fevered forehead.

Next time you hold a person's hands in yours, take a second to give those hands an extra squeeze. At the table, bless the food and the hands that prepared it. At bedside, fold your hands to pray. Use them lifted in worship or outstretched to reach for the moon. At the end of the day, put your hands to rest for work well done.

We can't all be Marthas, making candles from scratch, weaving our own baskets, or mixing our own dyes. But we are the hands of Jesus in this world. And that's far more important work.

Jesus, I want to use my hands the way you used yours to heal and lift and resurrect lost things in people's lives. I pray the compassion I feel in my heart will find its way to my fingers. Amen.

Never Cage Joy

Then he touched their eyes and said,
"According to your faith will it be done to you."
MATTHEW 9:29

The story is told of a Civil War battle in which a beautiful Southern mansion was used as a field hospital by the Union army. The plantation itself was a bloody battlefield, but the matron of the house refused to seek shelter elsewhere. She stayed in her home to organize medical supplies and help wounded enemy soldiers. She wiped their brows as they died. In the midst of this brutality, her courage and kindness were a testimony of grace.

Like this woman, but certainly in a less literal way, I have faced brutal circumstances that took possession of things I held dear and turned my life into a bloody mess. Unlike this woman, I didn't always respond graciously.

Sometimes I was slow to realize that my trials didn't define me. But eventually, I learned I am free, in Jesus' name, to behave with mercy regardless of my circumstances. I learned to ask, *What can I learn here? How can I help others?*

And when the sun is shining on my rooftop, when things are going my way? The same rules apply — and are just about as hard to learn. Our blessings don't define us either. We can't count on blessings; we have to hold them loosely. But we are free to behave with grace because of who we are, not what we have or what happens to us.

At times I've been like the little girl who set off to search for the bluebird of happiness. She looked in the past but couldn't find it. She looked to the future but couldn't find the bird. Then she looked in the present. When the bluebird of happiness appeared, she was happy. She felt inspired. She went out to do good while the bird sang a beautiful song in the treetops.

After a while, the little girl grew afraid. *What if I lose the bluebird of happiness?* she wondered. *What if it flies away?* So she built a cage of bamboo sticks, filled it with seed and pretty branches, and tucked the bird away for safekeeping. But the bird grew quiet, singing less and less until it stopped altogether. Eventually, the bluebird of happiness died.

The little girl learned that joy can't be contained but must be free to come and go, which it will—just as trouble is never permanent. In the Lord, I am free of circumstance, whether good or bad. At the beginning of each day I make two choices: first, to accept trouble if it comes and to look for opportunities to do good in spite of how I feel. Second, never to cage joy if it alights on my shoulder or lands in my lap. I will set the bluebird of happiness free to bless some other person's life. And sometimes the bluebird comes back to rest in my tree.

A neighbor of mine had lots of cats (at one time she had forty of them!). Since she was ninety-four years old, I sort of looked after her, doing her shopping, taking her to the doctor, and keeping her supplied with kitty litter. She died recently, and to my surprise, she left me two gorgeous diamond rings. That was totally unexpected. Thrilled, I had them sized and wore them proudly. Then someone pricked my happiness by saying, "Anyone with a tax-exempt, nonprofit ministry shouldn't wear expensive diamonds like that!"

The cutting words made me feel bad for a while. Then I let them go. They don't define me. I am free in Jesus. The diamonds? They were a bluebird of happiness passed along to me by a dear friend, and in that way, they were a gift from Jesus himself. (My husband, Bill, says I earned every sparkle in the rings for all the cat doo-doo I cleaned up.) For as long as I have the rings, they'll remind me of how God brings unexpected joy into my life. Should I lose them for any reason, that's okay too.

So if you see me wearing a couple of dazzling diamonds, let them be an encouragement to *you!* The Lord wants to bless you, unearned and unexpected. Accept the doo-doo and the dazzle that comes your way—you're bound to experience both!

Heavenly Father, although our lives are full of the unexpected, you are solid and sure. Help me to make my way through the mud puddles and to skip on mountaintops, taking things as they come. Bless me as the battle rages or the bluebird sings. Amen.

God's E-mail

I am in complete control.
It's the situation that is out of hand.

A little girl was learning the Lord's Prayer. Each night at bedtime her mother carefully repeated it. At last the child was ready to try it on her own. She knelt down, folded her hands, and began to pray. Each line was perfect until: " . . . and lead us not into temptation . . . but deliver us some e-mail."

God chuckles at our innocent mistakes. And he proclaims truth through children, because God does deliver e-mail—just when we need it most! The King of kings gives you and me access into his grace over the phone line of faith—direct to his royal chat room. His e-mail address is Jeremiah33:3@don'tstress.com: "Call to me and I will answer you and tell you great and unsearchable things you do not know."

Some of us are technologically challenged. I understand that. It can be intimidating to get into a brand new mode of communication when you're used to old-fashioned tools like telephones, typewriters, or even fountain pens. Once I sat down at a computer to log on to the Internet. The screen directed me to PRESS ANY KEY. I looked all over for the "any" key and couldn't find it!

I put my disk into the slot. Nothing appeared on the screen, so I called Computerland for help. The service department told me to put my disk back into the slot and be sure to close the door. I told the customer service guy to hold on. When I got up and closed the door to my office, the disk still didn't work. The screen scoffed at me, chiding BAD COMMAND, and called me INVALID. The serviceman said I shouldn't take it personally. But what was I to think? (Life was so much easier when it was just Dick, Jane, and Spot, wasn't it?) That afternoon, I went back to my dependable typewriter. My writing flowed. Now that is grace!

I am thankful that even when I don't understand the Lord or his ways (just like I don't understand the Internet), I can still depend on him by faith. When computers, calendars, and clocks seem to get the best of me and my time, I rely on the One who never changes. I figure God put me on earth to accomplish a certain number of things (right now I'm so far behind, I'll never die), but God is my hiding place from the tyranny of the urgent. Because of his grace, I can luxuriate in knowledge that all is well—even when the bits and bytes of my life look like scrambled gobbledygook.

The apostle Paul reminds us that through Christ, "we have gained access by faith into this grace in which we now stand" (Rom. 5:2). Like the Internet superhighway, we have access to grace at any time of day or night. This grace connects us with God himself and with people worldwide who have signed on to follow him. By faith we hyperlink to the wisdom we need to live by his kingdom principles. His extravagant grace is available in a fraction of the time it takes to go through the red tape of the Department of Human Services.

What is it you need today? Remember that you have immediate access to God's Riches At Christ's Expense (GRACE). It's all right there, waiting for you to dial in. Jesus said, "God's kingdom is within you." Click on that!

We throw open our doors to God and discover at the same moment that he has already thrown open his door to us. We find ourselves standing where we always hoped we might stand—out in the wide open spaces of God's grace and glory, standing tall and shouting our praise.

ROMANS 5:2–3 MSG

We're All Toads

Aren't you glad God loves us for what we are . . .
and not for what we should be?

Do you remember the story of the princess with the golden ball, and the toad who tormented her? In the popularized version of the fairy tale by the Brothers Grimm, the princess kisses the toad and voilà! The toad turns into a prince.

Most of us identify with the toad in this story, hoping to be kissed by a princess and be rescued from toad-ness. But that was not the original ending. In the original version, the princess gets fed up with the toad's demands, picks him up, and hurls him headlong against the palace wall. Splat! Encountering the wall—encountering truth—toad becomes prince.

An encounter with truth is what changes you and me into royal beings who are full of grace. And one of the most soul-transforming truths is looking in the mirror and discovering that we're ordinary toads—with warts just like everyone else.

I sometimes wear a little button that says, "Someone Jesus loves has AIDS." By wearing it, I remind myself that any kind of outcast deserves my compassion, not my judgment. Jesus said, "Don't condemn those who are down; that hardness can boomerang!" (Luke 6:37 MSG). We all have problems and hang-ups. Grace is at its best when it's shared with the least loved or most undeserving.

Have you ever considered that the very last words in the Holy Bible are about grace? The beloved apostle John's last recorded statement is, "The grace of the Lord Jesus be with God's people. Amen" (Rev. 22:21). John knew all about the "toad-ness" inherent in God's people. And he knew that what we most need in order to represent Christ on earth is grace.

Jesus knew that as well, which is why he modeled it for us in everything he did. He mingled with all kinds of people, and he loved them all. I wonder, did those who loved him back always go on to live triumphant, glorious lives? Were they always courageous evangelizers? Did each of their offspring grow up to be successful and popular? Did they overcome all of their personal weaknesses? What about the double minded Peter? The doubter, Thomas? The betrayer, Judas? Even Jesus was considered a criminal at the end of his young life. Does accepting Jesus as Lord mean that your life will be forever perfect?

In Jesus' day, many people believed sickness was a result of sin in a person's life. Religious people especially shied away from cripples or lepers, thinking they had brought misfortune on themselves. Whether or not that was true didn't matter to Jesus. He healed as many as called on him. He forgave them too.

The truth is, we are all born naked, wet, and hungry. Then things get worse. We all need grace at its best! Grace is simply knowing all about someone and loving them just the same. Jesus extends that grace to us every moment — and his Spirit in us enables us to graciously overlook the unbecoming, understand the unconventional, tolerate the unpleasant, overcome the unexpected, and outlast the unbearable in ourselves and other people.

Splat! That is grace in action. Grace is God's reality check in a phony-baloney world. When we no longer deny that we're ordinary toads, we don't need to judge anyone for living in a scummy pond instead of a palace garden, for we have been there too. We offer grace to all the way King Xerxes extended the golden scepter to Queen Esther as a token of acceptance and mercy (Est. 8:4). We don't have to patronize anyone. We just accept toads, lepers, the homeless, AIDS victims, the mentally ill, and our next-door neighbor.

Remember, friend, your arms are the only ones God has to hug other people, and he may want to use your lips to kiss a few toads. Let him. And pray that each time you err in discernment, it may be on the side of grace!

May the grace of the Lord Jesus Christ, and the love of God, and the fellowship of the Holy Spirit be with you all.

2 CORINTHIANS 13:14

Grace-full in His Sight

Hey, do you realize you are a miracle?
Someone like you will never happen again!

Have you ever meditated on Scripture by putting your name in place of the personal pronouns or characters' names? I love to go through my Bible that way. The Word of God just seems to come alive.

Take, for example, Genesis 6:8 (KJV): "But Noah found grace in the eyes of the LORD." Put your name in place of Noah's. How might embracing that grace change the way you pray? How might it change your day?

Find as many verses as you can about grace and insert your name into the flow of the Scripture. Here are a few to get you started:

My grace is sufficient for _____ (2 Cor. 12:9).
Grace is poured upon _____'s lips (Ps. 45:2 NKJV).
And great grace was upon _____ (Acts 4:33 KJV).

It is a great treat in my day when I imagine that God is seeing me covered, smothered, and smoothed over with extravagant grace. All my rough edges are rounded in grace. All my imperfections are hidden by grace. All my frayed ends are tied up with grace. All that I'm lacking is filled up with grace. How can I allow myself to fret and to worry, or to inflict guilt on myself, when I realize that in God's eyes I find grace upon grace (John 1:16)?

Don't you think we should delight in seeing ourselves the way God does? Then we can go out and share our best with the world. Our future is glorious in him because he has already said, "Have a good day and a fabulous forever!" He is growing us into saints. Though it may take a lifetime, shouldn't we rejoice along the way? Shouldn't we be grateful for how God is using us, even when the people around us might not appreciate it at the time?

My friend, remember to take this life one day at a time. When several days attack you, don't give up. A successful woman takes the bricks the Devil throws at her and uses them to lay a firm foundation. We all need enough trials to challenge us, enough challenges to strengthen us, and enough strength to do our part in making this a better place to live and love. Grace is receiving the gift of God in exactly who we are and bearing its fruit in the world. Just think how it changed the world because Noah didn't say, "I don't do arks." Moses didn't say, "I don't do seas." Paul didn't say, "I don't do letters." Michelangelo didn't say, "I don't do ceilings." Martin Luther didn't say, "I don't do doors." And, of course, Jesus didn't say, "I don't do crosses."

Some people can't afford the tuition for the school of hard knocks. But that's where grace comes in. When God believes in you, your situation is never hopeless. When he walks with you, you are never alone. When God is on your side, you can never *ever* lose. So don't be afraid of tomorrow—God is already there!

A darling woman wrote a letter to me about how finally, after many years of worrying about the unacceptable lifestyles of a son and daughter, she had learned to lay her son and daughter in God's hands. She wrote:

It seemed that forever all I did was beseech God's throne for these two. I read everything I could find on "letting go and letting God." At one of my lowest times, I told God that I needed to be ministered to . . . and for that one day I knew I could trust him to take over these children that we both loved. Then I decided to set aside Friday each week for God to minister to my needs. I turn over anything I'm concerned about for at least that one day. I dress as attractively as I can, put on my favorite perfume, and do everything that comes to my mind that I feel God leading me to do. I praise and thank him all day long. It was the beginning of the return of joy into my life.

Isn't this a beautiful idea? Remember, you are bathed in grace. Get dressed and put on your favorite perfume. God expresses his grace in the miracle of *you* every single day. You are grace-full in his sight. Believe it. Now go out and dance for joy!

"Hear the word of the Lord, *O nations; proclaim it in distant coastlands: 'He who scattered Israel will gather them and will watch over his flock like a shepherd.' . . . Then maidens will dance and be glad, young men and old as well. I will turn their mourning into gladness; I will give them comfort and joy instead of sorrow. I will satisfy the priests with abundance, and my people will be filled with my bounty," declares the* Lord.

Jeremiah 31:10, 13–14

Singing in the Rain

Grace is the ability to let your light shine
after your fuse is blown.

While flying to a conference recently, I was leafing through the airline's magazine which has items you can purchase through a catalog. I spied a darling ad showing a black umbrella. The description said, "Gray skies are gonna clear up!" The umbrella opened to reveal a blue sky with white fluffy clouds floating by. It was like moving out from under dismal rain clouds to a clear bright day at the touch of a button.

I had to order that umbrella, of course, because it was such an encouragement to me! When it arrived in the mail, it was even better than depicted in the advertisement. It brought inspiration and joy into my gloomy days.

None of us can avoid the gray skies and dreariness in life. At times we get absolutely drenched with troubles. But you know what? They're gonna clear up! Nothing lasts forever. The stuff we go through is only temporary. There will be lots of clearings along the way. And one day we will enjoy blue skies forever.

My new umbrella is in my Joy Room at home. I haven't had much of a chance to use it because in California our days are filled with so much sun and fun. But just like other people, I have my share of spiritual gray skies. When they come, I have to ask God to remind me that there is a clearing ahead. There is a bright shiny day coming. Soon enough, it will be time for a new beginning.

Each one of us needs a new beginning at some point or other. But it needn't come with a bang of fireworks or a streaking comet. New beginnings often come slowly. They may even sneak up on you — like a tiny ray of sun slipping out from beneath a black cloud. You can be inspired by the smallest things, so keep your eyes open.

Consider these: A tea kettle singing on the stove inspired the steam engine. An apple falling from a tree inspired the discovery of gravity. A shirt waving on a clothesline inspired the balloon. A spiderweb strung across a garden path inspired the suspension bridge. God will use the simplest realities to inspire something bigger and better in your life.

NBC news anchor John Chancellor once quipped, "You want to make God laugh, tell him your plans." God has much greater ambitions for us than we have for ourselves. He laughs at our paltry plans, then plots to surprise us with the greatness of his grace. Author C. S. Lewis referred to God's extravagant nature when he said, "You thought you were being made into a decent little cottage? God wants to make of your life a palace!" Of course, we have to learn to live with the rain and the fog while we're waiting for our skies to clear up and God's glory to be revealed. But rest your hope upon the grace that will crown your life when Jesus' plan unfolds. With the touch of a button he will draw you under the protection of his umbrella where you can enjoy sunny skies forever.

An optimist is someone who tells you to cheer up when things are going her way. I am more than an optimist. I have been ground in the mill, processed in the plant, and mashed like a potato. I am here to tell you that I am a firm believer in the Bible and its promises. I have learned that grace is not freedom from the storm, but peace within the storm.

So open your umbrella! Get out from under the downpour and remember the blue skies—they're on their way. In the meantime, by grace, you can celebrate the reality of God's extravagant plans for you and go on singing in the rain.

Set your hope fully on the grace to be given you when Jesus Christ is revealed.

1 PETER 1:13

"Show Me the Love!"

If you ever saw the movie *Jerry McGuire,* you'll recall the Oscar-winning performance of Cuba Gooding Jr., who played the high-flying, cocky football player Rod Tidwell. McGuire, a sports agent whose only client is Tidwell, is trying hard to land a deal for the athlete (who should be happy that *anyone* is willing to represent him).

In a memorable scene Tidwell makes it clear that the only thing that will convince him he's valued is cold, hard cash. "Show me the money!" he shouts — a challenge that became a popular mantra throughout America for months after the movie premiered in 1996.

I frequently hear from people who are baffled by a loved one's disinterest in the gospel or outright hostility toward Christians. "How can I witness to so-and-so?" they ask. "How can I convince people that they should give God a chance?"

And I wonder . . . are the people these folks are trying to "witness" to and persuade simply waiting to see evidence of the kind of love that is irresistible once it's experienced? Are they shouting inside, "Show me the love!"?

I know a lot of times it's not that simple. But, I believe, often it is. In his great treatise on love, the apostle Paul said, "If I speak in the tongues of men and of angels, but have not love, I am only a resounding gong or a clanging cymbal" (1 Cor. 13:1). Sometimes I wonder what the people we "love" are actually hearing when we're trying so hard to speak for God. Are they really getting the message that God's love is boundless, all-inclusive, personal, and lavish beyond description? Or are they hearing *Clang! Clang! Gong!*

In one of her many writings, Mother Teresa said,

> Be kind and merciful. Let no one ever come to you without leaving better and happier. Be the living expression of God's kindness: kindness in your face, kindness in your smile, kindness in your warm greeting.... To children, to the poor, to all who suffer and are lonely, give always a happy smile. Give them not only your care, but also your heart.

Sometimes it's easier to give someone "the answer" than it is to really give our hearts, isn't it? After all, they might reject our hearts. Better to just try harder to get our point across. After all, didn't Jesus say to go and "make" disciples (Matt. 28:19)?

Yes, but how did he intend for us to go about that great commission? "A new command I give you," Jesus said. "Love one another. As I have loved you, so you must love one another. By this all men will know that you are my disciples, if you love one another" (John 13:34–35). In other words, *show,* don't just *tell.*

I love how British novelist Anita Brookner describes "real love" as a pilgrimage. "It happens when there is no strategy, but it is very rare because most people are strategists."

Do we really need to try so hard to "get" people to "get it" (the gospel)? Or do we just need to show them the love? As Ruth Bell Graham so wisely reflects, "It's my job to love Billy. It's God's job to make him good."

In order to *show* love rather than just tell about it, Paul says that our love must be sincere. "Be devoted to one another in brotherly love," he says. "Honor one another above yourselves" (Rom. 12:9–10). Think about how you can do that today in the lives of the people God brings across your path. Keep it simple. It doesn't take a rocket scientist to figure out how to shower someone with the lavish love of God.

- Call someone who has enriched your life and say, "I'm so grateful for your friendship. Thank you for being you."
- Take to lunch someone you've been trying to "witness" to, and just spend the time encouraging her in the midst of whatever life is dishing out to her these days. Say, "I care. I'm here for you."
- Drop a pretty greeting card in the mail to someone you've been resentful toward and say, "I'm thinking of you and wishing you the very best today." (You'll be amazed at how your attitude will shift!)
- Tell someone who's done something nice for you how deeply you appreciate his kindness. *Show* him how grateful you are by doing something nice for *him*—not as "payment," but as an expression of the always abundant, lavish love of God. You can "afford" to share it!
- Simply walk in Christ's footsteps.

"Be imitators of God, therefore, as dearly loved children and live a life of love, just as Christ loved us and gave himself up for us as a fragrant offering and sacrifice to God" (Eph. 5:1–2).

Every time you interact with another human being, remember that their heart's deepest cry, like yours, is "Show me the love!" The apostle John makes it crystal clear: "This is how we know what love is: Jesus Christ laid down his life for us. And we ought to lay down our lives for our brothers" (1 John 3:16).

God showed you the love, lavishly. Now you show others, so they'll know whose you are.

How great is the love the Father has lavished on us, that we should be called children of God! And that is what we are!

1 JOHN 3:1

Love Everflowing

Every single minute of every single day, half a million tons of water wash over Niagara Falls. The everflowing river is a given. But in the middle of the night on March 29, 1948, the flow suddenly stopped. According to newspaper reports at the time, people living within the sound of the falls were awakened by the overwhelming silence. They believed it was a sign that the world was coming to an end. For thirty long hours they waited and wondered before the flow resumed.

What happened? Apparently strong winds set the ice fields in Lake Erie in motion. Tons of ice jammed the Niagara River near Buffalo and stopped the flow of the river until the ice shifted again more than a whole day later.

Talk about outlandish! No one would have, could have, ever predicted such a startling event. But life is full of outrageous surprises, isn't it? Some of them are delightful: like the box of ten thousand BBs my resourceful husband brought home for me when I needed only one to drop in my makeup bottle to keep it from getting thick and gooey.

But then there are those bizarre twists on our path that become our worst nightmares. Like the phone call I got in 1968 telling me my son Stephen had been killed in action in Vietnam. And the other phone call I got in 1973, informing me that my son Tim had been killed by a drunk driver. And the many phone calls I never got, for eleven long years, when my gay son and I were estranged, and I thought my heart was shattered beyond repair.

What I keep learning along this outlandishly unpredictable journey called life is: (1) we can't predict (or control) the unpredictable, so we might as well stick a geranium in our hats and be happy; (2) we can trust that nothing, absolutely nothing, can stop the flow of God's boundless love into our lives. No fluke in the weather or obstacle in our path can keep God's love from reaching us, even when the world seems to be coming to an end.

Trust me, I've been there. Trust Job, he's been there too. "Why did I not perish at birth, and die as I came from the womb?" (Job 3:11). Talk about a dark hour! Thousands upon thousands of people have "been there" — seemingly at that point of no return . . . frozen . . . out of the flow. But then, sometimes suddenly, most often slowly, they get back on center, "thaw," inch from despair back to faith, and stand strong again under the waterfall of God's everflowing love.

The apostle Paul, who certainly knew what it felt like to be out of the flow and at the end of his rope, summed up the bottom-line truth of our lives so beautifully when he recorded with utter confidence one of the most beautiful passages in all of Scripture.

Who shall separate us from the love of Christ? Shall trouble or hardship or persecution or famine or nakedness or danger or sword? . . . No, in all these things we are more than conquerors through him who loved us. For I am convinced that neither death nor life, neither angels nor demons, neither the present nor the future, nor any powers, neither height nor depth, nor anything else in all creation, will be able to separate us from the love of God that is in Christ Jesus our Lord (Rom. 8:35, 37–39).

Dear one, I urge you to read this love letter of faith and encouragement—the whole of Romans 8—over and over again ... and again ... until you become "convinced," with Paul, that *nothing* can stop the flow of God's tenacious, boundless, outlandish, wildly extravagant love into your life. So much in life is unpredictable, but God's love is certain.

The love of God toward you is like the Amazon River flowing down to water a single daisy.

Diamond Dust

A man was walking down the street when he passed a jewelry store. He stopped to admire some of the lovely pieces when he noticed the jeweler was preparing some stones. He watched him take uncut diamonds, which are yellow and quite unattractive, and place them in a machine. When they came out of the process the machine put them through, they were perfect, priceless diamonds.

This intrigued the man, and he entered the shop to inquire about this "magical" machine. The jeweler replied, "No, it's not the machine that works the 'magic,' it's what's *in* the machine: diamond dust. Only diamond dust can remove the ugly outer film of each uncut stone to allow the gem's brilliance to shine through."

When I heard that outlandish little story, I was transported back to a walk Bill and I took on the beach with some friends who own a cabin on the rugged coast of Maine. As we strolled along the shore, instead of fine sand we saw stones the size of tennis balls and others as large as basketballs. Yet they were all nearly perfectly rounded and smooth. The waves of the wild sea had transformed the once-jagged rocks into fine objects of beauty and wonder.

God works his outlandish "magic" on us in a similar way. Through the storms of life he transforms us into folks who are shaped in the likeness of his Son, who reflect his glory and shine like the precious gems he knows lie beneath what is unattractive in our appearance and behavior. We may wish for life's seas to be calm so we can live undisturbed, but God loves us too much to simply "leave us alone." When he sees our rough edges, he acts to remove them so we can become and enjoy exactly who we were created to be: his precious, beautiful jewels.

I know that if you're being tossed in the surf of life right now, these words can sound hollow rather than helpful. But that's why God has given us each other as we endure the storms of life: so we can "borrow" from each other's spiritual bank accounts of experience, hope, and faith when we're running low ourselves. Please, feel free to borrow from me! And from the many people who have walked the rocky shore before us.

The apostle Paul told us to "be joyful in hope, patient in affliction, faithful in prayer" (Rom. 12:12). Sometimes the only way to do that is to simply "set our jaw" and continue trusting that God *is* here helping us, molding us, working his magic, despite what seems scary or bizarre about the process. When we put ourselves under his care, trusting that nothing can come into our lives except through his filter of perfect love and wisdom, then we *can* be joyful, hopeful, faithful ... and ultimately transformed.

Does that mean we'll have no whirlwind emotions through all of this? Of course not. Human beings naturally become scared, angry, even ugly when they don't have control of what's going on in their lives. Even the most spiritually mature don't say, "Whatever, Lord!" without a few glitches now and then. But God can handle our thrashing about in fear and frustration, our crazy behavior when we don't get our way, even our fury at him when we're in pain and asking, *why?*

Madeleine L'Engle tells the story of one of her children when he was a toddler.

> [He] used to rush at me when he had been naughty, and beat against me, and what he wanted by this monstrous behavior was an affirmation of love. And I would put my arms around him and hold him very tight until the dragon was gone and the loving small boy was returned. So God does with me. I strike against him in pain and fear and he holds me under the shadow of his wings.

That little snapshot of the infinitely loving, patient, compassionate, protective God of ours encourages me to take my "dragony" self straight into his presence when I am the most afraid and, therefore, the most in need of love. As Paul says in Hebrews 4:15–16, "For we do not have a high priest who is unable to sympathize with our weaknesses, but we have one who has been tempted in every way, just as we are — yet was without sin. Let us then approach the throne of grace with confidence, so that we may receive mercy and find grace to help us in our time of need."

So if you're going through a stormy time in your life, realize with gratitude that our all-wise, loving Father hasn't deserted you. He isn't allowing you to be tossed about like those rocks on the shore of Maine for no reason. He is working with awesome skill to smooth your rough edges and bring forth from your soul the brilliant loveliness of Christ, "so that you may be overjoyed when his glory is revealed" (1 Peter 4:13).

And meanwhile, the doors to his throne room are wide open to you. You can run to him any time, even beat on his chest in fear and fury, and he will hold you close until the dragon is gone and the lovely woman returns.

He will sprinkle you with diamond dust until you sparkle with his loveliness. Now that's outlandish!

Joy is not the absence of suffering but the presence of God.

The Road to Hana

I heard a story about a traveling executive who phoned his wife from an airport telephone, concluded their conversation with a hasty good-bye, and replaced the receiver. Just as he turned to walk away toward the boarding area, the phone rang. *Uh-oh,* he thought, *probably the operator calling back to tell me I talked longer than I paid for.*

He grabbed up the phone, and indeed it *was* the operator. But instead of asking for more coins she said, "Sir, I just thought you'd like to know . . . right after you hung up, your wife said she loves you."

Makes me stop and ponder . . . How many times do I miss out on God's blessings, designed especially for me, because I'm simply not "present," too much in a hurry, or looking way ahead instead of close by?

Last year my husband and I were in Maui. We'd heard so much about the great road to Hana. "Be sure to make that trip," people told us. And as Bill and I drove around the island, we noticed T-shirts and bumper stickers that proclaimed, "I survived the road to Hana." Well, being tourists and doing all the right touristy things, we hopped into an open jeep with some friends and set out for Hana. We just knew it had to be a great place to end up, and we rode along with high hopes.

The road is long, winding, and narrow. There are lots of turnouts; we noticed pretty little spots with waterfalls and creeks as we zoomed past. We didn't have time to stop or look at anything, though, because we wanted so badly to *get to Hana.*

Well, we finally made it. We clambered out of the jeep with great anticipation . . . and got the shock of our lives. There were no waterfalls or sparkling streams. No cute little restaurants. No town. Just a few palm trees and a gas station. There was nothing to see in Hana.

Chagrined, we realized that the *road* to Hana is what we were supposed to be enjoying. All the little turnouts we'd roared past were where the treasures awaited us. We'd missed them all in our hot pursuit of our destination. Fortunately, there was only one way down the windy road, so we got to see all we'd missed as we flew by the first time.

Sometimes I feel like my life is the road to Hana. I am so busy trying to get to the end that I miss many of the little turnouts. Unfortunately, in real life I can't go back the way I came and see what I missed.

What might you be missing today? Right now, I encourage you to stop the "car" of your life wherever you are and take a good look around you. And *listen.* Is someone trying to get you a message? *I love you* is certainly one you don't want to miss! *I need you* is one you dare not miss, especially if you have a teenager in the house! *"I am come that they might have life, and that they might have it more abundantly"* (John 10:10 KJV, emphasis added). Jesus didn't say that just to hear himself talk; he means it! His lavish, intentional love is for *me,* for *you.* Right now, and forever.

Since that day in the jeep I've tried to pay a lot more attention to my journey rather than my destination. After all, I *know* where I'm going! Even though my limited human imagination can't begin to fathom Glory, Christ promises that I am sure to arrive. No need to hurry. I know that heaven will be far better than Hana could ever be, but right now I'm *here,* not *there.* So I am trying to really *see* the waterfalls and hidden treasures all around me, to *hear* the love messages God intentionally leaves for me as I follow the road toward Home. He has filled my journey with splashes of joy on a daily basis, if only I have eyes to see, ears to hear, and a heart willing to *stop* and say, "Thank you."

God has two dwelling places: one in heaven and one in a thankful heart.

Keep Sending Out Love

My son just doesn't call me the way he should. I'm lucky if I'm graced with a voice-mail once a month. Is it too much to ask to hear from my own son more often than that? I mean, I'm his *mother,* for Pete's sake." (I wonder who Pete is.)

This mom sounded angry. Her son had recently graduated from college and set off into the big wide world, but I knew she was hurting. I could see it in her eyes. *Doesn't he love me anymore?* I could hear her heart wondering. *Doesn't he recognize anything I've done for him? Doesn't he miss me like I miss him? Oh, how I miss him!*

Instead, out of her mouth came the petulant words, "Well, fine. I just won't call him back. I'm not chasing him down to get his attention. He can just see what it feels like to not hear from *me* for a long, long time. I'll give him some of his own medicine, see how he likes it." *Oh God, please let me hear from him! I miss him! I want my boy!*

Being a mother has its Hallmark card moments . . . and then it has its Far Side scenarios. Or worse. Someone has said, "Raising children is like being pecked to death by a chicken!" On those painful days, how tempting it can be to give up, retreat, and pout, or even strike back. But as a mother, there is simply no place to resign. (I know the lady who wrote that book; she is nuts but also an authority on the subject.) So trust me . . . you might as well kick back and enjoy your life! If your kid is "out to lunch" and forgets you for days or weeks, find another lonely kid and use your imagination to bring love into his or her life instead. So what if you don't get a birthday card from your daughter on time, or even a call to let you know she's arrived safely when you've been praying the whole day she's been at the wheel? I know it hurts, but how you *respond* will make all the difference—both in your own heart and in your relationship with your child.

Next time you're nursing your mother wounds, try something different. Something intentionally loving. Call *her* to see how she's doing, even if you can hear her eyes roll over the phone. Send *him* a note telling *him* that you love him, even if you don't get anything warm and gooey in return. I know you want more; sometimes you just wish you could turn back the hands of time and hold him in your arms like a baby.

I wanted more too. But when two of my sons were killed and a third was estranged from me for over a decade, I had a hard choice to make. Would I just put my mother's heart on the shelf and determine to stop this "loving" business because it was simply too painful, too risky? Naturally, I was tempted! I felt more than "pecked" by raising and losing children so dear to me; I felt sliced open (without any anesthesia), gutted, and left for dead. But God is in the resurrection business. He didn't want the mother's heart he'd planted in me to be sidelined or sealed up, even though he knew I felt I had good reason to cash it in on sending out any more mother's love into the world.

So he gave me an opportunity to keep on giving. A blessing in thousands of different disguises. I got to love other people's kids. Other hurting parents. Other devastated moms. Why did God do this? Just to keep on pushing me to obey his commandment to love, even though I felt like I was running on empty? Is that the kind of God we have — one who insists on using us up for his purposes without any regard to how we feel?

Absolutely not! He wants us to keep sending out love because he knows that when we stop, our hearts wither and grow hard. The soil that he longs to keep tilling and planting till the day we die becomes packed down with sorrow and bitterness, and we miss the harvest of all he has yet to bring forth in our lives regardless of our heartaches and disappointments.

God is never finished using us, but he is also never finished blessing us! No matter how grave our losses in this sin-strewn land we're passing through on our way to Glory, God's loving intention is to fill our empty arms, heal our broken hearts, and "replant" our barren souls. He can't do that abundantly if we close up shop on the loving business and hang our broken hearts on a hook somewhere in the back.

So do yourself a favor: Don't rob yourself (and don't let anyone else rob you either) of the abundance that belongs to you in Christ. Instead of giving up, keep giving out. Just keep sending out love. Keep planting and watering seeds. You may grow yourself a "blooming idiot," but don't stop being who God made you to be! Be glad for your mother's heart. Your love is special and powerful, like God's: "As a mother comforts her child, so will I comfort you" (Isa. 66:13).

Let God's motherly love wrap around your bruised and battered heart and comfort you until you are ready to send out love again.

Love is the fairest flower that blooms in God's garden.

Hooray for Gardening!

Old florists never die; they just make other arrangements.
Old gardeners never die; they just spade away.

You can't go into a gift store these days without running smack into all kinds of gardening paraphernalia. It's in your face: Stepping-stones that say, "Wish," "Imagine," or "Wonder." Little signs that announce, "Garden angel" or "Mother's garden." Birdhouses of every description—a boarding home advertising, "Cheap cheap rent," Italian bird-restaurants, log cabin respites for ol' fisher birds, and many other creative habitations.

Gardening fever is upon us. It seems as though everyone is a gardener, even if they live in a big-city apartment. Even if they have eleven green thumbs. Even if they wouldn't pull weeds for a million dollars. Even if they don't know the difference between a spade and a rake. Even if they hate vegetables and bugs, are allergic to bees, or have spring allergies. Suddenly everyone is a gardening maniac. Even I perhaps one day will burst my buds of calm and blossom into full-blown hysteria—even gardening hysteria.

Are you like me? Well, there are certain things anybody can plant—sweet Ps in a straight row, for instance: prayer, patience, peace, passion. But it's not enough for a gardener to love flowers. She also must hate weeds. As good plants grow, you pinch off bitter ones like panic, paranoia, and passivity. And by the way, while gardening, do squash pride. And please, lettuce love one another at all times.

We're all gardeners of the heart. Gardeners—because some ancient longing is built into us for the good, sweet earth. There is something evocative about the setting where Adam first met Eve. These two lovers walked with their Creator in the still of the evening as the Lord hit heaven's dimmer switch. There, at twilight, among the scent of roses and jasmine and apple blossoms, they savored a fellowship we can only dream about.

And wouldn't you love to have been in that garden outside Jerusalem two thousand years ago? The trees were budding, the flowers bursting through the ground. That morning as the sun was rising, Jesus wore his new body for the first time. In the hazy light of dawn he was mistaken for the gardener by a woman who had watched him die. Surely she never forgot that wonderful encounter in the garden.

Begin now to cultivate your half acre of love. All it takes is a few seeds no larger than grains of sand. Jesus said if you have faith no bigger than the size of a mustard seed, "nothing will be impossible for you" (Matt. 17:20). Remember when you were a child, you could buy a little necklace with a single mustard seed in a tiny glass ball? I had one of those; how insignificant that seed looked. Today I meet people whose lives flower with the results of tiny deeds of goodness planted year after year. The rest of us harvest the fruit from their lives. Often they haven't got a clue as to how God is using them. They weather storms and droughts and bugs and pestilence, just being faithful. They know that the blossom of a good deed fades with time but that the lasting perfume is the joy you receive from doing it.

The psalmist wrote, "Dwell in the land and enjoy safe pasture" (Ps. 37:3). A Chinese proverb says, "One who plants a garden plants happiness." An American proverb says, "One who plants a garden is not waiting around for someone else to bring her flowers." No, she is too busy picking bouquets to brighten the homes of everyone she loves!

If violets are God's apology for February, surely we can feed and groom and take a "start" of violet faith to everyone we know. Let the violet's deep blue color encourage you to keep believing, to wait for the promise of spring no matter how harsh the winter. Gardeners live by the signs of the seasons and know there is a time for everything, "a time to plant and a time to uproot" (Eccl. 3:2). They know there is a season for every color and taste. They know the brook would lose its song if God removed the rocks. They know rainbows promise enough rain and sunshine to grow everything in abundance.

Why the gardening mania? Why the books, calendars, accessories, decorations, tools, music, picture frames, furniture, clothes? Why are we so enchanted with white picket fences made into tables and chairs and headboards for the bed? Why the silk grapevines, sweet peas, and ficus trees for the bathroom, kitchen, and hall? Because we crave the sweet serenity of greens and golds and deep brown earth. Because fellowship with God began in a garden, and we long for that time and place. Because leaves quivering in the wind, blossoms nodding, grass ruffled by a breeze remind us of our real home and the peaceful destiny awaiting us. Because when I cheer up with my geraniums, smile at my pansies, laugh with my petunias, they teach me about God's big greenhouse bursting with joy.

For now, I'll take seedlings on loan from heaven and share the growth. Mint in the pot on my back doorstep perks up afternoon tea; I'll invite a neighbor to share it.

Bunches of parsley from the window box will flavor Aunt Sadie's stew. My pasta-loving daughter-in-love will relish fresh basil and rosemary. There are strawberries for Bill's breakfast, and rhubarb for Grandma's famous pie. We'll pick tomatoes for a just-out-of-the-earth salad to share with everyone on the block.

Gardening burns calories, lowers risk of heart attack, slows soil erosion, and provides shelter for a host of microlife. So hooray for gardening! Get your gloves muddy, your face tanned, and your knees crinkled here on earth. Nurture faith and love. Keep believing in the harvest. God will make something beautiful out of your effort and energy.

The most beautiful gardens bloom in the heart!

Now the LORD God had planted a garden . . .

GENESIS 2:8

Dear heavenly Father, thank you for making me a gardener of spirit. Help me sow kindness and reap blessing to heap into the lives of others. Amen.

God's Kingdom Fireworks

Enthusiasm, like the flu, is contagious—we get it
from one another.

For eighteen years our support group for parents of homosexuals has met monthly in a church across from Disneyland. Strangely enough, many of our members' children worked at Disneyland as those life-sized characters who walk around in costumes, signing autographs, and getting photographed with tourists. Last month our group was talking about this, and a new member, who'd been quiet the whole meeting, finally admitted she was Mom to a well-known character at another Los Angeles attraction. She'd been embarrassed to admit it until she heard everyone else's stories.

During the summer months our meetings are always interrupted by the 9:30 P.M. fireworks over Disneyland. For years it's been this way. Just when we're getting around to prayer, the exploding bangs and booms and rumbles start. I always thought, *Oh, my goodness, those fireworks; now we have to listen to that again!* I'd usually get irritated and annoyed—until one evening a couple from Iowa joined us. As soon as the fireworks started, they sat up, eyes twinkling. "Oh, the fireworks!" they exclaimed. There was wonder in their faces. They were excited and suddenly animated. "Can we stop for a few minutes to watch them?" they asked. "Imagine! Disneyland right across the street!"

The rest of us looked at each other and blinked. We had always simply "put up" with the noise. Suddenly, in our midst were two people helping us see it from a different perspective. To them the fireworks were not a problem but a possibility. Instead of feeling annoyed, they felt delighted!

Nothing has been the same since that couple from Iowa sat among us with their simple joy. Now when 9:30 rolls around, we no longer look at our watches and groan. Instead we look up with light in our faces, into each others eyes, and say, "Oh, the fireworks!" It's a reminder not to take our problems so heavyheartedly, a reminder to think of the possibilities within each problem and to know there is light even in the darkest sky.

Have you ever thought about how to recapture that precious sense of wonder?

Try this: Think of everything you normally take for granted. Make a list of the most ordinary, tedious things that happen every day over and over in your life. Now imagine a homeless man or woman coming to live with you for a day, sleeping in your guest room, showering in your bathroom, eating what you eat, going where you go. How do you think they would feel about this one day in a real house in a real neighborhood with a real family? What do you think they would say about the line of soaps and lotions in your bathroom cupboard? The ointments and medicines in your medicine chest? The linens and soft blankets? The furnace that blows heat through the floor?

Or imagine you died, then were miraculously brought back to live one more week on earth. What would you say? Who would you see? Where would you go? Experts say people who narrowly escape death look at things in a way the rest of us never will. Everything looks different, more vibrant.

"Oh, the fireworks!" The magic kingdom, the marvelous kingdom of our God, is right across the street regardless of where we live. When the parents of Disney characters come to our meetings, we give thanks and remember that Jesus loves their talented kids. After all, we are all characters out of God's great big book of tales, with our own gifts and eccentricities. We may as well get enthused and infect everyone we meet with his amazing love and power. Let the fireworks begin!

They recognized him . . . and they were filled with wonder and amazement.

Acts 3:10

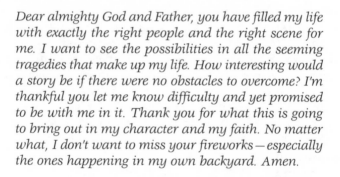

Dear almighty God and Father, you have filled my life with exactly the right people and the right scene for me. I want to see the possibilities in all the seeming tragedies that make up my life. How interesting would a story be if there were no obstacles to overcome? I'm thankful you let me know difficulty and yet promised to be with me in it. Thank you for what this is going to bring out in my character and my faith. No matter what, I don't want to miss your fireworks — especially the ones happening in my own backyard. Amen.

Nestle, Don't Wrestle

Most of us will miss out on life's big prizes:
the Pulitzers, the Heismans, the Oscars.
But we're all eligible for a pat on the back,
a kiss on the cheek, a thumbs-up sign!

Last year I watched Billy Graham being interviewed by Oprah Winfrey on television. Oprah told him that in her childhood home, she used to watch him preach on a little black-and-white TV while sitting on a linoleum floor. She went on to tell viewers that in his lifetime Billy has preached to twenty million people around the world, not to mention the countless numbers who have heard him whenever his crusades are broadcast. When she asked if he got nervous before facing a crowd, Billy replied humbly, "No, I don't get nervous before crowds, but I did today before I was going to meet with you."

Oprah's show is broadcast to twenty million people every day.

She is comfortable with famous stars and celebrities but seemed in awe of Dr. Billy Graham. When the interview ended, she told the audience, "You don't often see this on my show, but we're going to pray." Then she asked Billy to close in prayer. The camera panned the studio audience as they bowed their heads and closed their eyes just like in one of his crusades. Oprah sang the first line from the song that is his hallmark—"Just as I am, without a plea ..." — misreading the line and singing off-key. But her voice was full of emotion and almost cracked.

When Billy stood up after the show, instead of hugging her guest, Oprah's usual custom, she went over and just nestled against him. Billy wrapped his arm around her and pulled her under his shoulder. She stood in his fatherly embrace with a look of sheer contentment.

I once read the book *Nestle, Don't Wrestle* (by Corrie ten Boom). The power of nestling was evident on the TV screen that day. Billy Graham was not the least condemning, distant, nor hesitant to embrace a public personality who may not fit the evangelical mold. His grace and courage are sometimes stunning.

In an interview with Hugh Downs on the *20/20* program, the subject turned to homosexuality. Hugh looked directly at Billy and said, "If you had a homosexual child, would you love him?"

Billy didn't miss a beat. He replied with sincerity and gentleness, "Why, I would love that one even more."

When I related that comment to an audience of ten thousand people, they stood and applauded his words. The simplicity of his statement transcends our pettiness, heartbreak, and lack of clarity on an issue that polarizes and frustrates the nation and the church. The title of Billy's autobiography, *Just As I Am,* says it all. His life goes before him, speaking as eloquently as that charming Southern drawl for which he is known.

If, when I am eighty years old, my autobiography were to be titled *Just As I Am,* I wonder how I would live now? Do I have the courage to be me? I'll never be a Billy Graham, the elegant man who draws people to the Lord through a simple one-point message. But I hope to be a woman who is real and compassionate and who might draw people to nestle within God's embrace.

Any one of us can do that. We may never win any great awards or be named best dressed, most beautiful, most popular, or most revered. But each of us has an arm with which to hold another person. Each of us can pull another shoulder under ours. Each of us can invite someone in need to nestle next to our heart.

We can give a pat on the back, a simple compliment, a kiss on the cheek, a thumbs-up sign. We can smile at a stranger, say hello when it's least expected, send a card of congratulations, take flowers to a sick neighbor, make a casserole for a new mother. Do you know how to give a high five? Say "I love you" in language your teenager will understand? Back off even when you have a right to take the offensive?

Do you make it a point to speak to a person who shows up alone at church? Buy a hamburger for a homeless man? Call your mother on Sunday afternoons? How about picking daisies with a little girl? Or taking a fatherless boy to a baseball game? Did anyone ever tell you how beautiful you look when you're looking for what's beautiful in someone else?

Billy complimented Oprah when asked what he was most thankful for; he said, "Salvation given to us in Jesus Christ," then added, "and the way you have made people all over this country aware of the power of being grateful."

When asked his secret of love, being married fifty-four years to the same person, he said, "Ruth and I are happily incompatible."

How unexpected. We would all live more comfortably with everybody around us if we would find the strength in being grateful and happily incompatible. Let's take the things that set us apart, that make us different, that cause us to disagree, and make them an occasion to compliment each other and be thankful for each other. Let us be big enough to be smaller than our neighbor, spouse, friends, and strangers. Every day. Nestle, don't wrestle.

Offer your bodies as living sacrifices, holy and pleasing to God—this is your spiritual act of worship.

ROMANS 12:1

Almighty God and Father, how wonderful that you created us so differently yet each precious in your sight. Each one of us is the apple of your eye. Help me to be aware that the people you've put into my life are treasures. I pray for their salvation and well-being. Thank you for choosing me to love other people into your kingdom. Amen.

The Genius of Kids

A rt Linkletter to little girl: "What do you think we're supposed to learn from the Bible story where Jesus turned water into wine at the wedding?"

Little girl to Art Linkletter: "We learn that the more wine we have, the better the wedding!"

My husband and I recently watched a TV special that paid tribute to Art Linkletter's years producing *Kids Say the Darndest Things,* which was devoted to making kids and their conversations special. Bill Cosby was the host, and he began the program by showing fifteen hilarious video clips from Linkletter's original show. After each clip an individual was introduced — the same child all grown up, to greet Linkletter with a big hug! Was Art Linkletter surprised!

But that was the least of it. At the end of the program, Cosby announced that the studio audience was filled with folks who, as kids, had appeared on Linkletter's show. About four hundred people stood, holding children of their own or with their entire families! They were introduced to Linkletter as his face lit up with joy and amazement. He was overwhelmed with teary-eyed surprise. This man spent much of his life and talent infusing others with joy, especially children. Now the program managers had tracked down the kids he had interviewed from all over the country — to bring him joy. What a boomerang effect this had! Here was a man who enchanted us by looking at things from a child's point of view. Now grown-up kids trekked across the stage to greet him with huge smiles and embraces.

Kids are people who seem to pay as little attention to discouragement as possible. They catch a ray of sunshine and hold on tight. They are masters at the best kind of assertiveness—barging right into life. Kids know that a good laugh and a long sleep are the best cures for what ails you—and that you should never buy a coffee table you can't put your feet on.

If kids could tell parents the secret to raising them right, they'd say, "Spend half as much money and twice as much time on us!" They'd say, "Tickle and touch us more. Play with us, and then you can teach us anything you want." They'd say, "We're listening to everything you *don't* say. We're watching everything you do."

I heard about a little girl who lost her hair during chemotherapy treatments. When she came home from the hospital, her mother and father had shaved their heads to celebrate the occasion. I read about a boy who also lost his hair to chemotherapy, and all the boys in his class welcomed him back to school by shaving their heads too. This kind of object lesson speaks volumes to kids. Hard lessons and brilliant sacrifices say "I love you" more forcefully than all the toys or gadgets or treats in the world.

In *How to Win Grins and Influence Little People* (Honor Books) Clint Kelly gives parents great ideas. Here are a few.

- Grab your child in a bear hug and say, "You are a living miracle!"
- Ask your child to laugh for you, then say, "I love that sound. It makes me want to laugh too."

- Leave a note on the bathroom mirror: "Good morning, Brenda. What a fine smile you have!"
- Record your child's laughter and play it back once in a while. Say, "Now that's music to my ears!"
- Say, "You're so much fun to be with. Let's play!"

As a parent, you recognize your child's vulnerability. Knowing you could easily use it against them, you choose not to. Instead you find a way to honor their weakness and hallow their childish innocence. You fly the flag of joy from the castle of their life every day they live under your roof. You get down on their level and make sure you're having as good a time as they are.

Nothing is as precious as the giggles shared with a child. It's like the tinkling of a silver bell. Sometimes it's like a foghorn. But if your kids don't make you laugh, you're missing out on one of the biggest mother lodes in history. Maybe you need to loosen your collar and kick off your shoes. Take off anything constricting and uncomfortable. Pull out your bows and combs and rubber bands and mess up your hair. Risk a broken nail or two.

Why not try a few of these suggestions to become a child again?

- Go to a local park and feed the geese.
- Don't forget to take your toys into the bath with you, bubbles 'n all.
- Congratulate yourself on a job well done, with a gold star.
- Carry a bright, canary yellow umbrella on rainy days.
- Drink hot chocolate with marshmallows and whipped cream.
- Pray with the heartfelt sincerity of a child.
- Laugh and giggle often.

I found that time just went too fast with my sons. Before I knew it, two of them were gone. Before I knew it, there was not another chance to have a Jell-O fight in the kitchen, throw a few baseballs, or laugh ourselves silly over a prank. Martin Luther said, "If you can't laugh in heaven, then I don't want to go there." I'm looking forward to an eternity of laughing with my boys on the other side of the pearly gates. I hope the two waiting for me there are cooking up some crazy pranks to play on one another.

Keep happiness close to the surface of your life. If you're going through deep waters, financial trouble, serious stress at work, double deadlines, bitter blowouts with a spouse, it's even more important that you make yourself available to your kids — not just for their sakes but for yours. *You* need them. Don't pull away because you think you're no fun right now. You need their abilities to hope and to be happy.

Did you know researchers say that the simple act of turning your lips up (instead of down) stimulates good feelings? No matter how down you feel, how rotten, try smiling at yourself in every mirror you pass. First thing in the morning. Last thing at night. Broaden those luscious lips. Twist them toward heaven. You'll feel perkier faster if you smile than you would if you wallowed in gloomy thoughts. (Think of what your grandma used to say: "Imagine your face frozen into a frown!")

Then remember to *ask* your kids more than you *tell* them. Formulate a few prize-winning questions inspired by Art Linkletter, Bill Cosby, or Bill Nye the Science Guy. Resolve to find out what your child is feeling or thinking, with no preconceived notions of a right or wrong answer. Ask what she would invent if given all the money in the world to develop it. Ask her about her wildest dreams.

Ask her what she would be if she were a color, a wild animal, a member of the circus. Where would she go if she were a great adventurer?

Magic moments don't require special circumstances. You can tickle your kid when you tuck her into bed. You can kiss her toes and the tips of every finger. You can ask about her dearest wish when you're stirring the spaghetti or putting together a sack lunch. You find her soft spots easier when she's very glad or very sad. Tap into who she is at those times when she's not busy proving herself to you and everybody else.

Every time your child sees you happy and investing in her emotionally, you're binding her closer with invisible rope. If the rope starts to unravel, tie a knot in the end and hang on! Kids are like bouncing balls — they'll always take you by surprise. At least I hope they will. That's the way it's supposed to be. That's the way you maximize the joy.

Stay in the game. Don't ever give up. Twelve hugs a day — that's the minimum — don't have to be administered the same way twice. Keep up the attention. Let them know how cute you think they are. How smart! How witty! Let them know how much fun you think they are. Lay your head in her lap once in a while and listen. If she is not in a mood to talk, listen to her heart beat or stomach gurgle; if you can get close enough, listen to what she is thinking. Kids say the darndest things — in the most amazing ways.

To be in your children's memories tomorrow, you have to be in their lives today!

> Whoever welcomes a little child like this in my name welcomes me.
>
> MATTHEW 18:5

Dear Lord, how great it is, the way you made children the treasures they are. I applaud your creativity! Your sense of humor! Your love for life and humans like me! Thank you for the kids you have put in my life. I commit to receive the youngest, most insignificant, as I would receive you, were you to visit me. I love you Lord; give me grace to love little ones — and learn from them — the same way. Amen.

Unquenchable Grins

GIRL RECEIVES PIG-HEART TRANSPLANT; NOW SHE CAN'T STAY OUT OF THE MUD (actual headline, *Weekly World News*)

I spotted this headline as I was standing in line at the grocery checkout. Who makes these things up, anyway? What a blast it would be to work at that paper and come up with one bizarre headline after another. Their staff must have hilarious brainstorming sessions! And who buys this tabloid, anyway?

Some say truth is stranger than fiction; others say it isn't stranger, just more rare. One thing is sure: If you tell the truth, there's less to remember! Seriously, think of all the weird things that have ever happened to you and the people you know. If you've been through difficulties, as I have, try writing them into *Weekly World News* headlines like "Local Mom Goes Bald When Daughter Dates Space Alien." Go ahead, amuse yourself!

Then think about your life in politically correct terms: Do you know how you can tell if you're codependent? When you die, you see someone else's life pass before your eyes!

No matter what, don't ever let yesterday use up too much of today. If it sneaks up on you, turn the tables on it. Like interest rates, make trouble work *for* you, not *against* you. You don't always need a comedian to make you laugh. Once you get started, you can pull a few one-liners out of the bag yourself. When someone says, "Life is hard," say, "I prefer it to the alternative, don't you?" When somebody else complains about getting old, answer, "Right now, I'm just sitting here being thankful that wrinkles don't hurt!"

Life is too short to spend it being angry, bored, or dull. That was never God's intention. Maybe boredom and dullness aren't on any list of sins in the Bible, but they will sap your joy if you tolerate them.

Don't swallow Satan's lie that you have to keep swallowing bitter pills all your life. Fight back by developing and relishing a divine sense of humor, the gift God builds into your personality.

Got a problem? Make it an occasion to laugh. Live in a small town where everybody knows your business? Look at it this way: Even when you don't know what you're doing, someone else does. Concerned that your teenagers are never home? Try creating a pleasant and inviting atmosphere — and then let the air out of their tires. Worried about not being able to keep up with everything and everyone? Recognize once and for all that you're over the hill when you start spelling relief N–A–P.

No matter how old they grow, some people never lose their beauty. They merely move it from their faces into their hearts. According to psychologists, the happiest age is fifty. Perhaps by then we've learned to accept the fact that life is weird and things simply turn out as they turn out. No use sweating it. God uses all kinds of circumstances to tweak our lives. By age fifty we've pretty much decided that the second half of our life is going to be better than the first, because we like ourselves exactly as we are. Now that early baby boomers are turning fifty, surely there's a happier world on the horizon. Get ready to rock!

No matter how old you are, belonging to Jesus Christ means you've been given a heart transplant. With a new heart, he gives the power to be joyful, exuberant, and thankful. Eternal values replace temporary ones. He forgives our sins and rehabilitates our past. As a new creation in Christ, don't make the mistake of ruining the present by blaming yourself for past mistakes. God is a gentle heavenly eraser. He erases slowly sometimes but leaves no trace and doesn't tear the paper.

Our rebirth takes us to places we never dared to imagine. Regeneration catapults us to achieve things we never thought possible: to rejoice in suffering, be patient in adversity, love our enemies, do good to those who do us wrong.

We are going to inherit the new heaven and the new earth. If we could see now all God has planned for us, we'd be beside ourselves with anticipation and joy. We'd be going around with an unquenchable grin on our faces and a boisterous song in our hearts. Not deceived by pain, we'd be absolutely certain of our future. Our lives would inspire exciting headlines rather than dull platitudes.

To be in Christ is to live a life that is anything but a cliché. Watch out! God is making you authentic. Real. Rubbing off your fake fur. Changing your outlook. Giving you new desires. Making you marvelous. Fulfilling what you were created for. He is making you the "Queen of Quite a Lot," enlightening you for kingdom work.

Open your arms wide to God's imagination at work in you. Be brave. Then braver still. Never resist his insistence on your perfection. He is working all things together for good, not just for you and yours, but for people you've never met and may not meet until your paths cross in heaven.

So go ahead and imagine the way-out headlines your life may inspire in heaven. Envision your name in lights on the marquee of paradise. Then live it to the fullest. Get close to God and watch what happens!

You hem me in—behind and before; you have laid your hand upon me. Such knowledge is too wonderful for me, too lofty for me to attain.

PSALM 139:5–6

Father God, you know everything about me. Everything I'm thinking. Every detail of my day. You are changing me. Loving me. Leading me. No matter how boring my life gets, I'm in it for the long haul. I'm sticking with you, come what may. Amen.

Never Outgrow Motherhood

*Kids are like sponges—they absorb
all your strength and leave you limp, but give 'em
a squeeze and you get it all back!*

Every day is a happy-Mother's-Day for the children of moms who are elastic, who can stretch. Who but a mother puts up with cranky toddlers or irritable teenagers free of charge? Who else gets up to make her own breakfast on her birthday? Who changes the empty toilet paper rolls? Never tires of inquiring, "Did you flush?" Lies awake on Saturday nights listening for the last chick to return to the nest? Who gathers all her eggs, puts them all in one basket, and then gives it to God?

One day a mother was baring her heart to a friend, telling of a daughter gone astray. "If she were my daughter," replied the friend, "I would kick her out."

The mother thought for a moment, then said, "Yes, if she were your daughter, so would I. But she's mine, and I can't do that." That is how moms are.

Of course, we moms never live up to all the sentimental stuff said about us. We all have bad days. (You know you're having one, by the way, when you gently tuck the dirty clothes into bed and stuff the kids into the hamper!) The truth is that by the time you learn everything you need to know to be a mom, you're unemployed. But don't sweat it. Eventually you get to become a grandma, carrying pictures where your money used to be.

Be glad you have a stretchy, sticky mother's heart. Loving kids is not just about the kids. Raising one or two teaches you to manage crises and carry heavy loads in one arm while reaching out to someone else with the other. Pretty soon, walking the extra mile will be no biggie. Mopping up spills in other people's lives will become second nature. Let's face it: After raising two or three children, what could possibly "gross you out" anymore? (That reminds me of the mom who said, "I love to give home-made gifts; which one of my kids would you like?")

Every family tree, after all, has a little sap. Mothers get sentimentalized in pictures, books, and stories merely because they seem to glide effortlessly through any kind of upheaval. But it only *appears* effortless; really we're numb.

- We hang on so tight to hope — any last shred of it — that our fingers get callused; the soreness disappears.
- We know how to get out of tangles, because our children pull us into so many of them.
- We know how to mend a wounded heart, because ours has been broken several times.
- We know that the real art of raising kids is not only to say the right thing at the right time but to leave unsaid the wrong thing at the most tempting moment.

No, moms are not immortalized in literature and art because we are glorious creatures inherently good. The truth is, we've been knocked down and muddied more times than we care to remember. But we didn't stay down. Our love is tough and tender; if it weren't, we wouldn't be here now. Poets pay tribute to us precisely because our job is so tough. And that's what makes it so rewarding.

A wise man said that mothers are like Moses — "They never get to enter the Promised Land. Instead they lead others to a world they will not see." Let's face it: We can lead our kids to the borders of the Promised Land, but they have to go in and take the territory on their own. Worrying about them is like sitting in a rocking chair — it gives you something to do, but it doesn't get you anywhere. The years we have to shape their character are not many, but they are potent. The little moments — weighed together — impact everything our children will become. *Our* caresses become the way they treat others, *our* face the mirror reflecting their own, *our* arms the anchor that holds fast during their storms. Never mind the little boy who prayed, "Father, forgive us our trespasses, as we *give* it to those who trespass against us"; enjoy your children and teach them while they are still on your side!

Henry Ward Beecher wrote, "When God thought of mothers, He must have laughed. . . ." We might as well laugh too, dazed by how much there is to teach and how fast the time flies. Let's laugh at the ketchup on the walls and the smudges on the furniture. At the bats and balls and broken windows. At the goofy clothes in preadolescence and the lurches and lunges into independence later on. And let's not forget to laugh at ourselves. And keep laughing. Dance with joy and keep dancing.

You never know how God is working through your prayers or how he is using what you try to do, even when you don't see results. Live motherhood to the hilt. Bequeath your kisses and your discipline generously. Raise the standard of faith along with a finger to scold or correct. Spread your arms wide to a kid with a skinned knee. Lift a chin, hold a hand, tickle a foot. Keep the good times glowing. Make sure praise is flowing. You are a mother. Be glad!

> But his mother treasured all these things in her heart. And Jesus grew in wisdom and stature, and in favor with God and men.
>
> LUKE 2:51–52

Dear God, you know I feel so easily let down by my children, and sometimes I know I let them down. But they are treasures. I pray your will be done in their lives despite my failures or theirs. I want them to love you. Please hold them close. (Me too, Lord.) Amen.

Whatever, Lord!

*Part of learning "Whatever, Lord!" is accepting
the fact that there is a God, and I am not he.*

I was flying from Minneapolis to California, or so I thought, when the pilot announced we were returning to our port of departure. "Whatever for?" we all wondered, groaning and complaining. We were already three hours into the trip. The pilot explained that the aircraft couldn't get enough altitude to clear the Rocky Mountains near Denver. It sounded preposterous, since the flight routinely traveled west via Denver without a hitch. Despite our mutterings, we turned around and headed back to Minneapolis.

Once on the ground, I called my sister, who had taken me to the airport several hours earlier. She asked, "Where are you?"

"Back in Minneapolis," I surprised her.

"You should be in California by now! What happened?"

It wasn't long before the airplane mechanics found the problem. One of them had left a vacuum hose in the door, preventing the seal from being tight enough to allow the cabin to be pressurized and thus enable the plane to clear the Rockies.

A simple error by a careless mechanic drained the airplane's power to soar. As a result, over one hundred passengers had to go back to first base, unable to clear the obstacles in their path. Amazing what will keep us grounded, isn't it?

How like our daily lives, I thought, trying my best to laugh. I couldn't help but think of all the things that prevent me from soaring in the kingdom of God. What drains me of the Holy Spirit? What kind of vacuum hose saps me of strength and resilience? Okay, here's my list (you can make your own).

Failure to live with intention
Failure to love with abandon
Failure to practice prayer
Failure to walk to the edge of my faith
Failure to take one step more

I don't know about you, but I want to do more than survive life. It's not enough to just flap my wings a little before I hit the ground and get plowed under. I want to mount up like the eagle and glide over rocky crags, nest in the tallest of trees, dive for nourishment in the deepest of mountain lakes, and soar on the wings of the wind. I want to live at high altitudes, close to the Almighty. I want to try new things and sail over obstacles that loom on the horizon.

But there are challenges. I live with a medical condition that requires special effort to practice wellness. I am a wife, mother, mother-in-law, and grandmother. I travel frequently. I have to meet publishing deadlines. I am in my so-called soaring sixties, right up there with gals like Shirley Temple and Minnie Mouse! My life is full of high speeds and wild swings. I often need studied judgment on when to say yes and when to say no. It's so easy to let busyness bog me down.

I challenge you: What's your personal vacuum hose that keeps you from soaring? Go to the source. Think about what you can change. Pray for illumination. Let go of worry. Follow the disciplines outlined in the Bible. Communicate with the Pilot as well as the ground crew. You may have to retrace some steps to get it right. But it's worth it. Better than crashing and burning.

Live every day to fulfill your personal mission. God has a reason for whatever season you are living through right now. A season of loss or blessing? A season of activity or hibernation? A season of growth or incubation? You may think you're on a detour, but God knows the best way for you to reach your destination.

Get ready to take off. Climb. Ascend. Soar. Do whatever is necessary to remove the hoses that drain your energy or force you backward. When you do go backward, ease up, appreciate your fellow passengers, and take it all in stride, then get going again. Don't give up and take the bus. It's better to fly. Remember that whatever happens, you are not alone way up there, for "underneath are the everlasting arms" (Deut. 33:27).

> Praise the LORD, O my soul, and forget not all his benefits — who forgives ... heals ... redeems ... crowns ... satisfies ... so that your youth is renewed like the eagle's.
>
> PSALM 103:2–5

My heavenly Father, I want to use the few years you've given me to take flight in your kingdom. I'm going to live today as if it were the only day I had to live for you. Bless other people through my life. Amen.

Love More and Regret Less

Sometimes I make up my mind, other times my mind wanders,
and every so often I lose track of it entirely.

I read somewhere that very few brain cells actually disappear in midlife. But why then do I keep forgetting where I put my list of things I'll forget unless I write them down? I'm all for nostalgia, but it's hard to be nostalgic when you can't remember anything. At least memory loss helps me dispense with regret and guilt. I'm moving on, anticipating where I'm heading, open to today's answers to today's problems.

Some people pause to reminisce and then get stuck there. But I won't let my mistakes beat me up. So what if I missed while shooting for the moon? At least I journeyed for a while among the stars. And what if I did bite off more than I could chew? At least I cut a few wisdom teeth. Nowadays I may be slowing down, but I am definitely not settling back. I keep trying, just as my first-grade teacher taught me to do. And if at first I *do* succeed, I'll try not to look astonished.

How will the Lord use your life this year? This month? This day? Is there one thing you can do to make life better for someone else? Can you warm the home of an elderly friend? Chill out so a teenager can open up to your love? Knock on the door of a lonely single mom? Invite a seven-year-old for lemonade? The possibilities are endless. God expects us to use our brains and figure out what we can do to make a difference. Find out where he's working and join his crew.

When we bring sunshine into the lives of others, we're warmed by it ourselves. When we spill a little happiness, it splashes on us. Hope uncovers new possibilities and shows us what can be done. It wrestles with angels, looks impossibilities in the eye and winks. Hope springs eternal. Hope supersedes all good intentions.

Positive thinking, on the other hand, can get you only so far. When that train of thought won't get you further, jump track and keep going by the power of God's grace. After all, you know Immanuel, God who is with us. Dare to believe that he has planned greater things right around the corner for the ones you love. Hold your loved ones before the throne and count on God's answer in their lives. Don't let your ability or inability to think your way around circumstances hold you back. Pray and rest. Then pray some more.

Today make a decision to be less afraid than you were yesterday. To love more than last week. To regret less than last year. To move forward in good deeds. Be forgetful of the past. Remember to do all the good you can do in all the ways you can, ever as long as you can. And you can!

Now to him who is able to do immeasurably more than all we ask or imagine, according to his power that is at work within us, to him be glory.

EPHESIANS 3:20–21

Dear Lord, you are the great mind behind the universe. You made everything move according to your timetable and plan. Please forgive me when I fret and stew. Please help me move into my future, all the while helping other people and accomplishing your will. Amen.

The Boomerang Principle

Everybody wants to go to heaven,
but nobody wants to go there right away.

Don't we all want to live a long and happy life? We want as many years as possible to breathe, laugh, and work, serving God and praying for his kingdom to come. Along with this we'd like as many pleasant memories as possible, starting as early as possible. Youngsters, full of ambition, want to fulfill their destinies before the Lord returns. The middle-agers want to complete their lives' calling and make peace with troublesome people and issues. Older people want to see their lives come full circle before they die; they want to watch grandchildren grow up, graduate, marry, and have children.

No matter how old we are, most of us never really think of ourselves as old. Psychologists say most elderly people feel about thirty-two inside. (So Jack Benny was just a few years off!) Although our bodies betray us, our spirits often become more energized and focused as we age, and there is always too much left to do at the end of every life.

Somehow we must make peace with what we won't be able to accomplish. To do that, it helps to think of the things you probably can accomplish. What twenty goals would you like to reach before you exit planet Earth? If you are going to live until you die, you may as well arrange in advance for pleasant memories.

Every good life is a balance of duty and bliss. We will be called upon to do things we would rather not. Sometimes people say, "Just follow your heart," but that isn't necessarily the right approach. We have to weigh decisions by mind and spirit and by the Word of God. Whether you live to be nineteen or ninety, life is still short. Even the oldest, wisest man is amazed by its brevity. So make each year count. Instead of clutching it fast, give it away. "Cast your bread upon the waters" (Eccl. 11:1) and it comes back pretzels! That's the heart of the boomerang principle.

Do you have a gift for making people laugh? Writing a short story? Baking a great loaf of bread? Do you listen well? Throw a mean softball? Can you organize anything with flair? Are you good at making money? Selling just about anything? Running a race? Put yourself in the center ring. Offer your energy to life and do it heartily, unto the Lord.

Don't forget to celebrate anything you can think of. Do things that make you aware of how great it is to be alive. Every day is worth a party, not just the cookie-cutter moments. Special occasions are everywhere. Don't always be practical and expedient. God gave us license to be outrageously happy, friendly, and rejoicing.

- Celebrate your health, if it's good this month.
- Celebrate that you came through another year without a car accident.
- Celebrate wildflowers springing through the earth, the first robin in your yard, the first snowfall, the first good haircut you've had in years.
- Invite friends or strangers to celebrate with you. Look for original gifts you can give.

A couple of years ago a darling lady wrote to say she wanted to give me a birthday gift. For an entire year she would act as my "clipper." She was going to clip cartoons, articles, jokes, and other stuff for my newsletter, anything that would help my ministry. I thought, *What a wonderful idea.* So for several months I received a packet from her on the first day of every month. It was fabulous! All the cartoons and special articles came in so handy in putting together the newsletter.

Each month I eagerly awaited the packet, marveling at how she had taken the time to give me this special gift. Then suddenly the packets stopped arriving, and I learned that this thoughtful lady had died. But her idea blossomed. When my special doctor friend had his birthday that year, I was stumped about what to give him. Knowing he wouldn't need anything I could buy him, I decided that for one year my gift would be to clip out all the articles I could find relating to his specialty. In addition to his own studies, I thought he'd like to read what his patients were reading.

My husband got me a little clipping instrument to carry in my purse when I travel. I looked in magazines and newspapers for articles on health issues that would be of interest to my doctor. I found great articles and information at beauty shops or dentist offices too. Collecting the clippings in a bright neon envelope each month, I added enticing candy bars, sticks of gum, or whimsical candies so he had something to munch on as he read the material. Then I enclosed a funny card. My doctor enjoyed the package, and I learned a lot by investing my energy this way. It has boomeranged back into my life. What started out as a simple gesture to give has blessed and been a joy to me.

You can implement low-cost ideas to cheer the lives of people in your life: the baby-sitter, the postman, your favorite grocery clerk or carry-out boy. When you visit a home with small children, splurge on things that make kids' eyes shine. You don't even have to wrap them. Bring a deck of cards, a ball to toss, a Frisbee or jump rope. Get involved in their games.

Keep looking for ways to bless others. Compete with yourself to see if you can find more creative ways to love this week than last. Brainstorm blessing projects for next year. The point is to live every single day as though it were your last. Because if you do that, one day you'll be right!

He who refreshes others will himself be refreshed.

PROVERBS 11:25

Heavenly Father, help me not to count my days but to daily count the ways I can share life with other people. Amen.

All My Marbles

The end is not near; you must learn to cope.

Whenever my husband, Bill, and I travel to speaking engagements, we take along several pounds of iridescent glass marbles, piling them up in the middle of our book table. The marbles are actually flat, about the size of a half-dollar, with smooth, rounded edges. They come in rainbow colors: red, lilac, blue, amber, purple, and green. When placed in the light, the marbles reflect it and seem to shimmer, so we call them splashes of joy. In the middle of the marbles we put a small sign that says, "This is your free splash of joy. Place it on a windowsill where the sun will hit it . . . and it will remind you of all the places God wants to bless you!" There must be more than a ton of those sparkling iridescent splashes in circulation by now.

One day when I had finished arranging the table and was leaving to take my place on the podium, I said to the volunteer selling my books, "Remember, the splashes of joy are free; everybody can take one." Later when I returned to the book table, I saw dozens of ladies in the foyer walking around with my book *Splashes of Joy in the Cesspools of Life*. I thought, *Wow, that book certainly sold well today, but I wonder why so many people bought that one?* (I had seven others on sale too.)

Noticing five or six empty boxes under the book table, I asked the volunteer about it. She said, "Oh, you said all the *Splashes of Joy* were free, so I let everyone take one!"

Uh-oh!

I hope those *Splashes of Joy* became showers of blessing to the many who picked them up that day. I did laugh about the incident . . . later, that is. Joy really is a take-it-or-leave-it kind of thing. My glass marbles remind me that the choice is always mine. I can choose whether to shine and sparkle or sit and stew.

Whenever child star Shirley Temple got up to perform, her mother would always say, "Sparkle, Shirley!" And (since I'm the same age as Shirley) I took those words to heart. That day at the book table I heard the Holy Spirit whisper, "Sparkle, Barbara, sparkle!"

When the devastating earthquake struck southern California in 1994 (they said it wasn't the "big one," but it was big enough for me!), one woman wrote to tell me how her little "sparkle stone," as she called it, helped her keep smiling through her tears. She wrote,

> About a year ago I attended a retreat where you were the speaker, and you gave each lady some sparkle stones to take home and put on a windowsill. I did. Then I kind of forgot about them. But their message of Jesus' love came to me as I was cleaning a huge mess of broken things after the earthquake.
>
> The refrigerator and all the cupboards had opened and emptied, and everything had broken into millions of pieces. I was sad, scared, and upset as I cleaned. Then I saw a "sparkle" among my broken treasures. I cried as I scooped up the little sparkle stone and thanked God that I had been able to

have those treasures for the years I had enjoyed them. I thought, "For this I have Jesus." When I saw that sparkle stone, I had to smile and say, "Thank you, Barbara, for this reminder that Jesus loves me. I'll sparkle for him."

Remember this story; don't miss the beautiful colors of the rainbow while you're looking for the pot of gold at the end of it! When your life comes to a close, you will remember not days but moments. Treasure each one. And know that the most glorious of these are not the so-called moments of success and accomplishment, but rather those moments when out of dejection and despair you let rise within you the promise of joy!

The glass marbles we give away remind me why I go out to speak: We are put on this earth not to see through each other but to see each other through. I want to help see others through their pain. I want to throw a little encouragement party. I want others to be drenched with joy. That's what makes it all worthwhile.

When the marbles are first shipped to me from the manufacturer, they are bundled in small nets and covered with a powder residue that prevents them from scratching during shipping. If I want them to be lustrous and transparent when we hand them out, I have to undo each bundle, place the marbles in the kitchen sink, rinse them off, then spread them out on a towel to dry.

One day when I was home, busy at this task, a newspaper reporter called. She said she was calling various authors to find out precisely what they were doing at that exact moment. Wondering how this was going to sound, I answered, "Well, I'm washing my marbles—in the sink."

The reporter didn't answer for a moment. Then she asked, "Who is this again?"

"It's Barbara Johnson."

"The Christian author?"

"Well, yes!"

"And you're washing your marbles?"

By this time she must have thought she'd dialed the wrong number and reached the home for the hopelessly bewildered. But she laughed as I explained that I always rinse the splashes of joy before giving them away. Then I told her that washing my marbles helps me remember how God washes us and cleans us up. His love rinses away the residue we pick up trying to protect ourselves from life's scratchy circumstances. When he is finished with us, we are shining, transparent, and lustrous.

Many of my friends know I love to joke about my marbles — about washing them and occasionally "losing" them. In fact, one friend sent me a little plaque titled "All My Marbles Certificate." It said, "This is to certify that I, Barbara Johnson, am in possession of All My Marbles. I can never again be accused of not having All My Marbles." At the bottom of the certificate, this zany friend had written, "If everyone had All Their Marbles, the world would be a nicer place to live!"

Sometimes I do lose my marbles; my mind wanders — or it leaves completely. But that's okay. The marbles I have left remind me of the light of God's plan and how wonderful it is to be alive. I've decided to enjoy today's moments today, because someday today will be a long time ago. I know a lady whose mother died in her arms of breast cancer shortly before this lady herself was scheduled for a double mastectomy. A survivor of breast cancer for several years now, she says with a smile, "Even on bad days, I am so happy! To think I'm even here to have a bad day cheers me up!"

Certainly the rain falls on the just and the unjust (chiefly on the just, because the unjust steal their umbrellas). But a few splashes of pain don't get me down for long. In the cesspools of life, I remember the colorful splashes of joy on my windowsill. I take my rainbow with me and share it with others! We cannot protect ourselves from trouble, but we can dance through the puddles of life with a rainbow smile, twirling the only umbrella we need—the umbrella of God's love. His covering of grace is sufficient for any problem we may have.

> Cleanse me with hyssop, and I will be clean; wash me, and I will be whiter than snow. Let me hear joy and gladness. . . . Create in me a pure heart, O God.
> PSALM 51:7–8, 10

Dear Lord, you have sprinkled splashes of joy throughout my moments and my days. When I look back, I see your patterns of color and meaning, shimmering just like a rainbow. You are beautiful, God, and you make my life beautiful too as you wash me whiter than snow. Amen.

Birthday Countdown

The scary thing about middle age is the knowledge
that you'll soon grow out of it.

Andy was miffed when he didn't get the part he
wanted in the Christmas pageant. He had hoped for
the role of Joseph but got stuck being the innkeeper. So
Andy decided to pull a fast one and get even with Joseph
when he came with Mary, looking for a place to stay.

"Come right in, folks," innkeeper Andy told them.
"I've got plenty of room."

Perplexed, Mary looked at the startled Joseph, who
quickly rose to the occasion.

"Hey, this place is a real dump," he said, poking his
head inside. "I'd rather go out and sleep in the stable."

Whatever happened to the wit and wisdom that
served us so well as kids? Why can't we use that when
middle age baffles us? Experts say innate creativity
begins to disappear at about age eleven because we stop
using it. We become progressively less curious and spon-
taneous.

Youth is not a time of life but a state of mind. It boldly
takes risks, seeks adventure, hopes for the best, and dis-
plays courage. You are as young as your faith is strong.

The actor Jimmy Stewart stayed young until the day
he died at age eighty-nine. Although extraordinarily talented, he remained touched by the fact that he was a

celebrity. One time a stranger put his hand out and said, "Mr. Stewart, I don't guess it means much to you, but I want you to know I think you're wonderful." Taking the man's hand to shake it, Jimmy held on to it tightly, looked him in the eye, and said, "It means everything to me."

We live out the kingdom of God within us when we treasure each other like that and when we find ways to turn unfortunate things around. Laughter is one of those ways. Laughter stirs the blood, expands the chest, electrifies the nerves, and clears the cobwebs from the brain. If you laugh a lot, when you are older all your wrinkles will be in the right places!

If you live to be one hundred, your heart will have beat 3,681,619,200 times, pumping 27,323,260 gallons of blood weighing over one hundred tons. (If you end up tired, you've earned it!) Think about making every heartbeat a happy one.

Actually, I think living to be one hundred would be great, but living to fifty twice would be so much better. The way to do that is to get one year younger each year after your fiftieth birthday. So on your fifty-first birthday you turn forty-nine, at sixty you are forty, and so on. I'm not saying lie about your age; actually grow younger every year!

The first rule for this (you'll start looking younger too) is to scatter joy to everyone you meet. There is no more effective beauty secret. The second rule is to exercise regularly—and the best heart workout is reaching down and lifting someone else up. The third and last rule is to guard your enthusiasm; in fact, let every experience in life multiply it. Every single experience! If someone leaves you only the shirt on your back, you have a choice: You can either use it for a crying towel or make a sail out of it. Go sailing, not ailing! And on your adventure at sea remember that the pessimist complains about the wind, the optimist expects the wind to change, but the spiritual man adjusts his sail.

One way of adjusting your sail as you travel through rough seas is to find fun in unlikely places. Sometimes you have to give yourself permission to have fun. You cannot trap fun like an animal or catch it like the flu. But if you go looking for it, it'll come. The magic of fun lies in the unexpected — whether chasing dreams, flying kites, or going up on the down escalator. Break out of your middle-age mold and become a little bit crazy — even if friends think you're fresh out of a rubber room!

You can't turn back the clock, of course, but you can wind it up again. As a recycled teenager, insanity may be your best means of relaxation. The secret of growing younger is counting blessings, not birthdays. Don't grow up; grow down. You'll know you're getting the idea when you begin buying cereal for the toy, not the fiber.

If you keep it up long enough, sooner or later you'll grow down from teenager to toddler. Uh-oh, there is one thing about being a two-year-old that could take all the fun out of getting younger. Beware the toddlers' creed: *If I want it, it's mine. If it looks like mine, it is mine. If I take it away from you, it's mine. If I had it a little while ago, it's mine. If I give it to you and change my mind, it's mine.* No wisdom there; this breaks every rule of growing down. Skip this stuff, then hop and jump to infancy — that blissful time when you have no more responsibility than to eat and sleep and bask in the love of your family. No one will blame you for an occasional wakeful night or fussy afternoon. Dependent on others, enjoy the minutes as they fall through the hours, on your way through eternity.

Do not worry about your life. . . . But seek his king-dom, and these things will be given to you as well.

LUKE 12:22, 31

Lord, show me how to become like a child again. Let's go roll in some meadows and giggle like a brook. Teach me the quiet simplicity of loving you. Amen.

Making Life Bearable

I wonder . . . do kamikaze pilots wear helmets?

I grew up taking risks. In fact, I've always thought success and risk go hand in hand. My motto is that people who live in a dangerous world ought to live dangerously. Of course I don't advocate taking foolish risks, but neither should we play it so safe that our lives are boring and our spirits dull.

Most of us are bombarded by daily warnings: buckle up, button up, watch for bumps ahead. We need brake checks, breast checks, dental checks, and Pap smears; medical insurance, disability insurance, life insurance, car insurance, mortgage insurance, and nursing home insurance. On and on. If we were to do everything everybody told us, we'd spend every minute of our waking day trying to prevent calamity.

I figure you may succeed in living longer if you are willing to stop doing everything that makes you want to live longer. I once knew someone intent on living forever, a vegetarian nonsmoker who moved to the country, where there was plenty of fresh air, healthy water, and no industrial waste. Sadly, he died in a car accident when he was only thirty-eight. The real tragedy is not that life ends so soon but that we wait so long to begin it.

Life *is* dangerous. All of us are on a kamikaze mission. Not one of us will make it out alive. Should we wear helmets?

I don't know about you, but I refuse to play it safe. I'll drop goodness and joy as many places as possible before my time comes to say *sayonara*. The best any of us can do is to show unconditional love to family, friends, and strangers. The best we can do is to encourage faith without excluding fun and laugher, and to bring the gospel and the love of Jesus into the lives of everybody we meet.

The best we can do is to live until we die, a life that is bold and true and fun. Maybe that's why I've put bears on my stationary. I send out so many notes — short, encouraging messages to people going through long, discouraging trials. Scripture tells us to bear with one another (Col. 3:13) and to bear one another's burdens (Gal. 6:2). On my notes, one bear is hugging another, and the logo says, "I wish I could hug away your hurt, but I hope it helps to know I care." I hope the bears remind everybody that nothing in this dangerous world is unbearable, because the Lord promised not to give you more trouble than you can bear (1 Cor. 10:13).

Worry never empties tomorrow of its sorrow, but it does empty it of its strength. Don't let anyone rob you of your confidence in God. Know his Word. Hold on to his hand. He will make your impossible mission possible and your life so much more than bearable.

> For he will command his angels concerning you to guard you in all your ways; they will lift you up in their hands.
>
> PSALM 91:11–12

Dear Lord, your own Son lived dangerously so I might enjoy abundant life. Help me to live that life to the full, gladly embracing the risks you place in my path. Amen.

The Big Joy Room— In the Sky

My idea of housework is to sweep the room with a glance.

Whenever I'm not on the road, the things that consume me most are the mail and the telephone. Mail to Spatula Ministries is collected in large rectangular tubs that we pick up at the post office. (Our address should be a P.O. *tub* number rather than a box number because *box* doesn't begin to describe the barrel-size bin where our mail ends up.) I try to respond to letters with a phone call because it's so much faster. At the same time, I exercise on a bike set up in my Joy Room, a room filled with anything funny I've ever collected or been given: plaques, toys, gadgets, hats, and goofy things. Right in front of my bike I've posted a large map of the U.S. As I cycle, I mark my progress by sticking a pin into the map every twenty-five miles. That way I take imaginary trips across the country while talking on the phone, answering letters in a roomful of joy-filled gizmos!

My life is filled with people now, just like it was when I was at home rearing four boys. At that time I started a practice of taking the first day of each month off, making it a day just for myself. I still do this and find it helps me keep everything else in perspective. Just knowing I have one day a month all to myself keeps me grounded and motivated.

Still, there are days when I start feeling blue. On those days I've learned to avoid certain things. I won't weigh myself, listen to sad music, get a haircut, open a box of chocolates, or shop for a bathing suit. Instead on such days I make it a goal to perk up and be happy. The best way is to become a joy-germ carrier. Infecting people with joy so they break out in symptoms of laughter — that's the very best way to beat the blues.

My joy habit has turned into a hobby. Sometimes I think up crazy bumper sticker ideas inspired by crazier ones like this: "Husband and dog missing. Reward for dog." Other times I create cards with uplifting themes. As my friend Faye Angus says: "We can't all be stars, but we can all twinkle." Or I might just call a friend and ask profound questions:

Would a fly without wings be called a walk?
Is it possible to be totally partial?
Do they sterilize needles for lethal injections?
Can you be a closet claustrophobic?

Women love jokes about dieting, aging, and men (those creatures God gave to us so we'd always have something to laugh about). These have become favorite themes for me to write and talk about in a spirit of fun. When I travel, I combine all three themes, struggling to eat sensibly despite lavish hotel menus, keeping up with schedules made for twenty-year-olds, and flying cross-country with my husband, Bill, at my side. Both of us have learned to laugh about things that go wrong along the way, realizing that life is nothing at all like the brochure.

I've made it a habit to wring out of every single day all the fun and love I can find. If you don't know where to start next time you're feeling low, take it simply:

7:00	Get up, don your makeup, and dress up for breakfast.
8:00	Show up for work with a big smile on your lips.
10:00	Take a coffee break and pass out crazy-flavored jelly beans.
12:00	Invite a friend to lunch.
2:00	Call your spouse, a child, or a friend and make a date for the weekend.
4:00	Order a bouquet of flowers to be delivered to your neighbor's door.
6:00	Put candles on the dinner table and turn on the music.
8:00	Design a funny card and send it to your aunt or mother.
10:00	Belt out your favorite gospel song in the shower and memorize a Scripture promise before you turn out the light.

After you get the basics down, you can fill in the hours with crazy excursions into comedy. You'll learn what makes people laugh and how to communicate through chuckles. The point is simply to get started. The point is never to give up. The point is to be friendly and to focus on the person next to you. There are two ways to come into a room: "Hey! Here I am!" or "Oh! There you are!" People who like people are people that people like! It's as simple as that.

One of the best ways to encourage someone who's hurting is with your ears—by listening. But it's so much harder than talking. And few people do it well. A good listener not only is in demand everywhere but after a while actually knows something.

Mother Teresa pointed out that the great tragedy of life is not hunger or disease but feeling unwanted. This tragedy is as prevalent in America as in India. Everywhere, abandoned, isolated people ache with loneliness. As you're rushing through life, take time to stop a moment, look into people's eyes, say something kind, and try to make them laugh! Tell them life is easier than they think: A person need only accept the impossible, do without the indispensable, bear the intolerable, and be able to smile at anything!

Recently Bill and I stayed at a lovely old bed-and-breakfast inn loaded with antiques. In our room, hanging by the bed, was a long stick with a sort of bellows on the end. The hostess told us it was a quilt fluffer. You slide it inside the covers and pump it a few times to make the bed softer. Maybe we all need something like a quilt fluffer to buoy up our sagging, smashed-down world. We've been sitting on each other far too long.

Try it. Fluff things up a bit or pretend for a moment that you're a star—then go ahead and poke a hole in someone else's darkness!

> That they may be encouraged in heart and united in love, so that they may have the full riches of complete understanding, in order that they may know the mystery of God, namely, Christ, in whom are hidden all the treasures of wisdom and knowledge.
>
> Colossians 2:2–3

Dear heavenly Father, surely your kingdom will be like a great big joy room where we will gather with you. Meanwhile help me to cast the bread of happiness and laughter on the waters of this world. I love you and wait expectantly for the adventures you send me to. Amen.

Crazy Quilt

I love you more than yesterday.
Yesterday you really got on my nerves!

I like to think of my family as a big, beautiful patchwork quilt—each of us so different yet stitched together by love and life experiences. We are different textures: smooth and soft, rough and sturdy, bright and sparkly, subdued and peaceful. If one square is worn, others are there to hold the quilt together.

Patchwork blankets tell stories. How many women have treasured the work, passing it from generation to generation? The blue patch may have been the pocket of Great-Grandmother's dress, the tiny square of pink from the blouse of an aunt who died of smallpox, the little triangles of corduroy from the knickers Great-Uncle Joe wore playing that newfangled game called baseball. What transpired in the family while the blanket was being pieced together? Were they traveling west on a wagon train or huddling before a coal fire in the Appalachians?

Family quilts are an affirmation of the past, present, and future. They reassure us with their warmth and comfort us with memories of hard times that turned out well.

For generations mothers and grandmothers have given a cherished quilt to daughters on their wedding days. Quilts symbolize the heritage of home passed on, the fabric and threads of one life continuing into the next.

Sometimes we dream of how we want our family quilt to look. We choose certain colors or patterns or thread and start to work. We know we want it to be something unique and wonderful. But somehow life shuffles everything around. We lose this but find that. One piece doesn't fit, so another takes its place. The threads get tangled, and we have to snip and start over or work the tangles into the design. The quilt we envisioned is not the quilt we hold in our lap. It's turning out differently. The miraculous thing about being a family is that in the last analysis, we are each dependent on one another and God, woven together by mercy given and mercy received.

Sometimes family seems more like a crazy quilt than a carefully designed patchwork. We learn to love each other better through the crises that shape our lives. Through the odd bits and pieces of my own life I've learned a few truths that I've stitched into my crazy quilt. Truths like the appropriate temperature in a home is maintained by warm hearts, not hot heads. A grudge is much too heavy a load for anyone to carry.

Some quiltmakers work a deliberate "mistake" into each quilt as a symbol that nothing is perfect. It's a grand idea that comes from living simply and close to the earth. And these quilts are some of the most highly prized throughout the world. Each one is different. Each one is valuable.

Perhaps if we are capable of creating the warm refuge of a family quilt, we may also have the stuff to spin a cocoon and then make a butterfly. While waiting for heaven, let's keep putting those pieces together, stitching them carefully with love and kindness into a patchwork that only we can make.

But seek first his kingdom and his righteousness, and all these things will be given to you as well.

MATTHEW 6:33

Dear Lord, thank you for the quilt of my family. With all its contrasting patterns and frayed edges, as well as its joyful colors, it is the most beautiful thing I've ever seen. I'm so glad for each person you've given me. Thank you that we belong together. Please bless us, Lord, everyone. Amen.

Spread Your Joy

Your face is a billboard advertising your philosophy of life!

Lord, make me a nail upon the wall. . . ." That's the way one woman's prayer began. A nail. Common and small. "From this," she continued, "hang a bright picture of Thy face." She prayed that others might see Jesus in her.

Recently while traveling to Yucaipa, California, to speak at a women's retreat, I began complaining about how tired I was of sharing my story. My friend Lynda listened as I spoke about how difficult it was to tell the same story, the same gruesome details, over and over: the death of two of my sons, the third son's disappearance into homosexuality, my husband's terrible accident. I didn't feel like spreading any joy that day, because I didn't think I had any to spare. I felt burned-out, exhausted, and empty.

Just then a huge billboard zoomed up out of nowhere, standing beside the highway. In letters ten feet tall were the words SPREAD YOUR JOY, an advertisement for a local church. Like a bolt of lightning, its message struck me to the core. I had not wanted to tell my story one more time, to share the joy I found learning to accept life no matter what. Was it just a quirk that the sign appeared at that exact time and place on the highway to Yucaipa, of all places? Was God encouraging me to be faithful?

Lynda burst out laughing. Surely God had heard our conversation! The conference turned out to be fabulous; I'd rate the results at 110 percent! My energy was high, and there was joy in abundance. Many women came forward for prayer; some even gave their lives to Christ for the first time. In sharing my life and the joy God placed deep within (so deep I barely knew where it was anymore), God had restored my own joy.

By choosing to get up on a platform and do what God had called me to do, I was acting as a nail upon the wall of the kingdom of heaven. My story is such a small and insignificant thing compared with many other stories of faith and the story of Jesus himself. But I chose to stay securely fastened on his wall, holding his picture in place. And you can too.

Don't get me wrong. I usually don't get billboard messages from God. He doesn't often interrupt my whining with a giant highway sign! He doesn't zoom in on me with a telephoto lens when I feel tired and beat. Life is mostly just getting in the car or on another airplane, climbing the steps to one platform at a time, and faithfully holding his picture in place—whether I feel like it or not. But there is the secret: As we do the thing in front of us, joy comes. It multiplies and eventually hits us smack between the eyes, like a boomerang. It becomes a "hallelujah" in the choir loft of our mind. Joy is a treasure that multiplies by division.

Don't ever abdicate God's call on your life. Too often we expect someone else to fill in for us. We're too tired, too old, too busy. Someone else can fill our shoes, we say. Someone else can do the job. Truth be told, someone else has been relied on far too long, for far too much. It's time we stood up and helped shoulder the burden. Give your gifts, your story, your fortune. Turn the basket upside down and shake every crumb loose. Pour out the vessel. Dump the bucket. Empty your pockets. Tomorrow or the next day or the next you'll have more than ever! Don't give up. Spread your joy!

> Being confident of this, that he who began a good work in you will carry it on to completion until the day of Christ Jesus.

PHILIPPIANS 1:6

Lord, on my darkest days help me not to give up or hang back. People are waiting to see your face, to know your faithfulness, to experience your joy. Make me a nail for your picture fastened in place. I surrender my reluctance, even my unbelief. Help me to spread joy! Amen.

God's Spiritual Stove

Evangelism is no more than one beggar telling
another beggar where he found bread.

It's a cold day. It swirls snow, kicking up a storm. Icicles
dangle from the nostrils of every rainspout. I breathe
arctic vapors, shiver, and blow steam through chapped lips,
beating hands together for a smidgen of warmth. Have you
noticed in cold climates how people seem to hibernate
during the winters? It takes something extra to stick to the
job, keep your kids happy in the house, get to church, and
be a good neighbor in those frosty winter months.

We experience frigid temperatures in our faith too.
There are cold days when hope dies: love walks out the
door, a friend moves out of town, the job ends, the bank
fails. God seems distant. Prayer fades in your throat
before you barely utter a word. The Bible stares back with
a blank page. You might call it spiritual frostbite. It is
painful. Poisonous. Dangerous.

The church is God's spiritual stove. In its containment
we pile on fuel, stir the embers, strike a match. James
indicates that if we say, "Keep warm and well fed" and do
nothing tangible for people who are cold and hungry,
there is no profit in it (James 2:16). We need each other's
warmth to survive the winters of our lives. We need a
place to thaw, even a handout sometimes, if only in the
form of encouraging words.

Henry Ward Beecher stopped to talk with a newsboy on a blustery morning. "Aren't you cold?" he asked. The boy answered, "I was until you came, sir." To a soul that is starved for human kindness or warmth, even a casual but personal question can be life-giving, because it shows you care.

You are a member of Christ's body, the church. Will you warm someone else today? People who get snowed in while mountain climbing are instructed to build an ice cave, keep their boots on, and lie down next to each other, sharing the heat of their bodies in order to survive. When you warm someone else with a smile, a hug, or pat on the back, you receive their warmth back. We comfort one another "with the comfort we ourselves have received," wrote the apostle Paul (2 Cor. 1:4). "If two lie down together, they will keep warm. But how can one keep warm alone?" said the preacher (Eccl. 4:11).

Stand by someone who is standing alone. A single woman or a lonely teenager out there aches for someone to put an arm around them and squeeze tight. Unless you've been there, you have no idea how good that feels to a person who gets little or no affection. Not everyone has a spouse, parent, or friend who offers physical touch, but everybody needs it. Experts say twelve hugs is the minimum daily requirement.

Someone once said, "I know I'm not what I should be and I'm not yet what I'm going to be. But I'm not what I was—I'm on my way because you touched me." Touch someone with a warm word. There are people who are subject to other people's complaints all day long. Give a compliment or friendly greeting to a store clerk, janitor, nurse, or office manager. Their ears are hungry for something positive, encouraging, and healthful to the spirit. See what a variety of loving phrases you can offer that will bring a smile to the face of people you meet. Challenge yourself! Make a game of it. Just bring joy today.

A little girl was late walking home from school one day, and her mother was angry and worried. The girl explained that her friend had tripped on the sidewalk, stumbled, and broken her doll on the way home. "Well, did you stop to help her fix it?" asked the girl's mother. "Is that why you're late?"

"No, Mommy, we knew we couldn't fix it, but I stopped to help her cry."

In the extreme cold of life we need each other. Don't be fooled by the façade of strength that some put on to protect themselves. Put a little May and June into someone's life. Don't hide behind propriety. As the U.S. Army admonishes, "Be all that you can be." As your kindergarten teacher taught you, "Be a buddy." Look both ways—who needs a hand, a word, or one of your ears for a few moments? Lending yours might mean making someone's day. Reach out and warm a heart!

An anxious heart weighs a man down, but a kind word cheers him up.

PROVERBS 12:25

Lord, someone I'll meet today is lonely or afraid. Give me your words to bring that person comfort, courage, or calm. Help me warm a friend or stranger who is tired and cold. I want to be a harbinger of spring. Amen.

Waterproofing Life

Jesus didn't say, "Let your light so twinkle."
He said, "Let it so shine!"

Human beings thrive on laughter. Since most of us can't afford vacations in Hawaii, we have to learn to make our own fun. The best way to do that is to keep your state of mind green and golden: find, recycle, or produce joy wherever and however you can. A good humorist is a work of heart! The Hasidic Jews believe that the best way to worship God is by being happy. They incorporate dance and celebration into their spiritual walk.

Today make yourself a joy box and start collecting things that make you smile or laugh. First you'll need a shoe box. Then you might want a basket. Later a barrel. And before you know it, you may have to add a room onto your home, as Bill and I did in order to have a place large enough to hold everything. My Joy Room has become a haven to many others who just need a place to kick back, put life in neutral, and smile again. Just sitting in there is a form of therapy. Even the clock seems to chime out the message "I love you, friend!"

Having returned at one point in time from the black pit into new life, I feel I have earned this joy room, where the walls are filled with laughter. One of the things I treasure most is a wooden plaque inscribed with the name "Barbara" and its meaning: "Coming with joy." I'll never forget the woman who said to me, "I feel like I'm living in a parenthesis—the horrible parenthesis of life!" I know how she feels. You try to get ahead of that closure, and the way out escapes you. You feel closed in, trapped in an emotional closet. I've found that "coming with joy" into the lives of people who feel trapped helps free them. Each time someone laughs, the raw edges heal, the rough ache subsides.

Sometimes you have to hunt and peck for things that hit your funny bone. You can even find something to laugh at in the Bible, for the Bible is like the ocean—you can wade in it, feed from it, live on it, or drown in it. Here's what some kids wrote after studying the Bible:

- Noah's wife was called Joan of Ark.
- Moses went to the top of My Cyanide to get the Ten Commandments.
- Joshua led the Hebrews in the battle of Geritol.
- David fought the Finkelsteins, people who lived in biblical times.
- The people who followed Jesus were called the Twelve Decibels.
- The epistles were the wives of the apostles.

Humor is the chocolate chips in the ice cream of life. Remember the old-time Good Humor Man who drove his ice-cream truck down every street in the neighborhood, chiming a jingle on those hot summer days? All the kids came running as soon as they heard the sound. But good humor doesn't drive down many streets anymore. You have to go out and get it. Fortunately, it's not that hard to find.

One woman told about buying a new pair of Gore-tex boots. Wearing them for the first time, she came across a puddle and quickly avoided it. She didn't want to get her brand-new boots muddy. After dodging several puddles, she suddenly realized why she had bought the boots in the first place! The next puddle she came to, she stepped in lightly. The next one she plunged into. The next she leaped into with the enthusiasm of a two-year-old. By the time she got home, her boots were caked with mud, her feet were dry, and her heart was happy.

Humor is the waterproofing of life. With it you can take on all the mud puddles life puts in your way. Don't avoid them, don't step lightly through them. Jump! Splash! Dare them to defeat you. God promises a safe landing, not a calm voyage. He restores to you the joy of your salvation. Nothing, not even the worst sin (or mud!), can separate you from him.

Remember, when you fall down, you gotta giddy up! Rise to the occasion. And rise early for the sheer joy of it. The Bible says joy comes in the morning (Ps. 30:5). Abraham rose early to stand before the Lord (Gen. 19:27). Jacob rose early to worship the Lord (Gen. 28:18). Moses rose early to meet God on Sinai (Ex. 34:4). Joshua rose early to fight for the Lord (Josh. 6:12; 8:10). Ezekiel rose early to receive the word of the Lord (Ezek. 12:8). Jesus rose early to speak with his Father (Mark 1:35). God's loving kindnesses and compassions "are new every morning" (Lam. 3:22–23).

"Thou shalt not wallow in it," says the *Humor Gazette*. Get up early and get on with life. "He will yet fill your mouth with laughter," says Job (8:21). The psalmist wrote, "My mouth is filled with your praise" (Ps. 71:8). Don't settle for chortles or giggles. Go for the guffaw! Why settle for twinkle when you can shine?

A little boy looked out his window at bedtime and saw the crescent moon. "Look, Daddy," he said. "There's a smile in the sky." Yes, there is! Not only in the moon but in the stars. Jesus is the "morning star" (Rev. 2:28). Someday the trumpet will sound, the dead will rise, and we will be caught up to meet him in the skies (1 Thess. 4:16–17). If that doesn't make you smile, I don't know what will!

> In the same way, let your light shine before men, that they may see your good deeds and praise your Father in heaven.
>
> MATTHEW 5:16

Dear Lord, sometimes it's not much fun here on earth. But I am committed to joy. Full and everlasting joy. Show me how to find it or create it. Show me how to fill the lives of others with the happiness that comes from knowing you. I love you, Lord! Amen.

The Messages of Hands

You can't climb the ladder of life
with your hands in your pockets.

Hands are silent couriers carrying messages from our hearts. They open doors to bid you welcome. They push a swing for a laughing youngster. They gently brush away tears of pain. My hand on your shoulder offers compassion. A handclasp conveys strength and courage. A wave of the hand says good-bye to a friend or beckons a stranger who is lonely. An infant delightedly curls his dimpled fingers around my wrinkled ones. No words are spoken. None are needed.

We use our hands in so many different ways. Here's the way one missionary woman used hers: first to bake missionary cake, then to write the recipe so *we* might enjoy it.

Prepare fire in mud stove. Rinse utensils with boiled water. Check flour for bugs. Measure and sift flour and sugar. Stop to kill cockroach crawling across the table. Add two eggs. (Oops, none left; have Johnny fetch from tribal neighbors.) While waiting, pull lizard out of grass hut roof and throw outside. Crack eggs. (Uh-oh, they're duck eggs. Use anyway; who's going to know?) Add lemon juice. (No lemons; substitute papaya juice.) Stir. Put in greased pan and sprinkle with palm nuts. Bake until cake rises. Serves a family of six or a few hungry village children! (Adapted from Mrs. Joy Benzio, Trans-World Radio Headquarters.)

You can do loving things with your own hands today: organize a drawer, pick a bouquet of wildflowers, write in your journal, draw a picture card for a child, pat a puppy, braid a little girl's hair, make a batch of cookies, decorate a wall or a shelf, pinch a cheek, pull some weeds, wash your husband's car. The boomerang joy in all this is that the hand that gives, gathers!

One day I was in a Thrifty Drug store. Because the name of our ministry is Spatula, I am always on the lookout for cheap plastic spatulas to give away. My supply was low and the spatula I had been using at meetings looked more like a kitty litter scooper. That day in Thrifty I saw a salesgirl kneeling down and sorting through a large box of kitchen utensils. Among them were brightly colored plastic spatulas for only fifteen cents apiece! I excitedly asked if I could sort through the utensils with her, picking out all the spatulas. I found about thirty and gleefully loaded them into my shopping cart. "I am so happy," I told the cashier. "Do you have any idea how hard it is to find such *nice* spatulas so *cheap?*"

She shot me a funny look as she swooped up my cartload of spatulas and stuffed them into a sack. I figured it was more fun *not* explaining what I wanted them for.

I took those thirty spatulas and passed them out as a cheerful reminder that we use our hands as well as our hearts when we rescue a friend, sister, or neighbor when she's hit the ceiling and has to be scraped off. In God's big kitchen, these handy utensils can be used for so many things.

Remember, God provides the ingredients for our daily bread but expects us to do the baking. With our own hands!

May the favor of the Lord our God rest upon us;
establish the work of our hands for us—yes, establish the work of our hands.

PSALM 90:17

*You are almighty God, and yet you allow me to be
your hands and feet on earth. How priceless that you
anoint me for ministry using my own two hands.
Thank you, Lord. And show me how much I can do
with what you've already given me. Amen.*

Anticipate the Best!

We spend our lives dreaming of the future,
not realizing that a little of it slips away every day.

When my publisher called one winter morning to tell me that sales of my book *Stick a Geranium in Your Hat* had reached one million units, the head of the sales department invited Bill and me to fly to the company headquarters, all expenses paid, for a big blowout celebration. "Oh, that won't be necessary," Bill, my homebody husband, assured the executive. "Barb and I can just celebrate at home."

That afternoon he left the house whistling a merry tune and wearing an assured expression on his face. He was a man with a mission, setting off to create a celebration suitable for marking this unexpected accomplishment. While he was gone, my mind was filled with fantasy, wondering what he would bring home as his surprise for me. I pictured something sparkly, maybe a ring with a gem, or a little diamond bracelet. When he'd been gone more than two hours, I imagined him speaking to the mâitre d' of some fancy restaurant, setting up a lavish meal to celebrate this special occasion.

Just as I was about to burst with excited anticipation, Bill walked in the door, still whistling but now wearing a look of smug satisfaction. "Here you are," he said proudly, handing me a plastic grocery bag. "Two bundles of fresh asparagus. I know how you love it."

I looked in the bag. Sure enough. There were two perfect green bundles of my favorite vegetable. Bill had spent two hours driving from store to store, trying to find this out-of-season delicacy. "It's pretty expensive this time of year," he said, beaming, "but I figured you deserved it."

"Thanks, Mr. Wumphee," I said, more than a little surprised to be receiving asparagus instead of *carats* but genuinely touched by his thoughtfulness. "That was really nice of you."

Sometimes anticipation builds up our expectations to nearly bursting—and then reality sets in and our expectations fade out like the sorrowful sound of steam escaping from a cooling kettle. That's what happened when our four boys were young and we all piled into the family car one summer to drive from our home in southern California to visit relatives in Minnesota. On the edge of the desert, about eighty miles from home, we passed an unusual motel that caught the boys' attention. The "rooms" were shaped and painted like colorful wigwams or teepees, and the boys thought it would be the greatest thing in the world to get to spend the night there and sleep in one of those wigwams.

They were so excited about it that I promised them we would spend the night there on our way back home, even though it was less than a hundred miles from our house. They eagerly predicted how much fun it would be to sleep in such an unusual place, how it must look inside, where each of them would sleep, and what it would be like to tell their friends they had slept in a wigwam. Throughout the trip they reminded me of my promise. There was no way I was going to drive by that place on the way back without stopping!

Finally we headed home, and by the time the wigwam hotel came into sight, the boys were beside themselves with anticipation. "We're there!" one of them shouted as soon as the long poles poking out of the roofs appeared on the horizon.

I checked us in, and the boys scrambled out of the station wagon and soon were fighting over who got to hold the key and unlock the wigwam door. But as soon as the door swung open, the boys' faces fell.

The room was cramped and dark. The carpeting was threadbare in some spots, crusty in others. The window-unit air conditioner that protruded from the wall had long ago given up on cooling the 110-degree desert air, and there was no TV or even a bathroom—just a sink in one corner of the room. We would have to traipse one hundred feet away to a community bathroom.

It was one of the longest nights our family ever endured, with all our hot, sweaty, unbathed bodies crowded into that hot, windowless room. We were so eager to get out of that awful place that we were all awake before dawn, and for once the boys were actually waiting in the car before I even had the suitcases loaded.

When I think of the way eager anticipation has ended in disappointing reality so many times in my life, I'm thankful to remember that there's one place I can antic-ipate going to that will be even *better* than I expect. I can't even imagine all the wonderful things that are waiting for me there. And I know my home is there, prepared for me, grander than anything on earth, because God him-self has told me so. With all my heart I long to be there, safe in God's heaven, singing praises with his angels, thrilled beyond earthly imagination to be in his eternal presence.

I hope to see you there!

No eye has seen, no ear has heard, no mind has conceived what God has prepared for those who love him.

1 CORINTHIANS 2:9

Dear heavenly Father, help me see the bigger picture. When people and things disappoint, I know there is a grand plan with a higher purpose than my pleasure. If I wait, I will know joy that never quits. Help me lean into your will and be filled with your presence in the meantime. Amen.

Those Struggle Muscles

If I had my life to live again, I'd make the same mistakes,
only sooner.

Children need to experience small failures and setbacks so they can learn how to pick themselves up and try again. We all have struggle muscles to develop. If you constantly take care of problems for your kids, you will train them in weakness, allowing their character to atrophy.

The great president Theodore Roosevelt, described as "a steam engine on two legs," was asthmatic as a little boy, not expected to live beyond age four. In the middle of dark nights, when Teddy would gasp desperately for breath, his father would pick him up and carry him outside—walking around for hours or riding in the horse carriage. In the arms of his father the small boy felt safe. The choking subsided as he gulped in fresh air and rested against a strong shoulder. His father was always there, protecting and nurturing him.

But the day came when Theodore Sr. took Teddy aside and told him, "Beating this thing is up to you now, son. Your mind is strong, but you need to develop your body." His father helped Teddy live an active life involving strenuous exercise, outdoor activities, hunting, and sport of all kinds.

Teddy threw himself into everything with determination and abandon. As he grew taller, his chest expanded and his neck thickened. He disciplined his mind and body. He was developing struggle muscles on his own. Years later those muscles helped him survive life's tragedies. Brokenhearted as a young adult by the death of the father he adored, the dark night came when both his beautiful wife and his mother died within hours of each other. Teddy left Boston and headed for the Badlands of North Dakota, where he took on the rugged life of a mountain cowboy. Although a refined Easterner, Teddy gained the respect and admiration of the toughest men riding the range. Today his granddaughter says, "If it were not for that Badlands experience, he would never have had what it takes to be president."

Our lives seem ordinary compared with Teddy Roosevelt's. But are we really so different? Think of the way our heavenly Father carries us through the hard times, providing comfort in those gasping, choking moments, helping us to breathe again. As we survive and grow, he challenges us to take up the fight ourselves, providing the tools to flex and grow strong. Do we do our part, trusting his Word, continuing to practice the spiritual disciplines? Do we work to the maximum of our ability? Are we determined to fight the good fight of faith?

Some say Teddy never got over the death of his wife and his mother. And yet, developing his struggle muscles in the Badlands, he went on to remarry, father six children, and lead a great country through some of the worst years of its history. We can be paralyzed by our setbacks, angry and bitter, or challenged by them to make the world a better place. The trouble with people today is that we have too many cabooses and not enough engines. Teddy was an engine. He wanted to stand in his father's shoes, so he used the tools his father provided to defeat adversity. He made sure the shoes fit.

Several years ago Oprah Winfrey got rid of an entire wardrobe; one woman bought a pair of her four-hundred-dollar shoes for five dollars. Later that same woman told Oprah she was having a difficult time raising her children on her own, but then she added, "Sometimes when I feel I can't make it, I go in the closet and I stand in your shoes."

We may feel small and spiritually asthmatic, but God is there, allowing us to grow our struggle muscles. He knows we'll need them to live out the glorious destiny he has planned for us. He has already dreamed up a great dream and a brilliant future for us. But to fulfill our potential, we need to be strong enough to fight, overcome, and love others into his kingdom.

So go for it! Lift those spiritual weights. Box with the phantoms that haunt your soul. Run hard. Get used to rough riding in Satan's badlands. Don't be afraid of mistakes or defeats; they are building blocks for all your successes. Remember, determination and faithfulness are the nails used to build the house of God's dreams.

> For I know the thoughts that I think toward you, says the LORD, thoughts of peace and not of evil, to give you a future and a hope.
>
> JEREMIAH 29:11 NKJV

Dear Lord, sometimes I feel so weak, but I refuse to give up. Please help me know your presence. You are running alongside me. You love me enough to allow me to struggle for muscle. Then I will be strong and you will lead me into your great dream. Amen.

Humble Joy

My karma just ran over my dogma.

In this crazy world it's nice to know that some people still perform commonplace work with dignity, holding the world together with old-fashioned, down-home virtues. Examples are all around us. Folks still hold tight to faith in hard times. And when life pours success upon them, they just continue on, humble and kind.

It had been a long night of painting for Precious Moments artist Sam Butcher. As daylight brought busloads of tour groups to the Chapel in Carthage, Missouri, many people recognized the artist at work and began asking for his autograph. After several hours of signing, Sam finally climbed into his car and headed home through the rain.

Just outside the Precious Moments property he spotted a van on the road. Several women were standing beside it, staring dejectedly at a flat tire. Sam pulled in behind and got out to assess the situation. They needed a different jack, so he got one from his trunk and sat down in the mud to change the tire. The driver explained she had brought her church group all the way from Pennsylvania to see the Precious Moments Chapel "down the road."

"Have you ever been there?" she asked.

Sam nodded.

The lady said, "This has been a perfect trip except for one thing. Just as we were ready to leave, we learned the artist was signing figurines. We wanted so badly to have some things signed, but the lines were long and we couldn't get near him. We just had to get back home. Now here we are with a flat tire!"

"That's too bad," Sam said, finishing his work. "As soon as I wipe my hands, I'll be happy to sign anything you have."

The lady's mouth dropped open. "You?" she exclaimed. "You're the artist Sam Butcher? Why would an important person like you stop to change a tire?"

Sam replied, "Because it's flat!"

Obligingly he signed each item they handed him, leaving the ladies smiling in the rain. That flat tire had boomeranged on a group of women from Pennsylvania—and brought them joy.

Anytime we stop to care for others in their trouble, we carry the opportunity to bring boomerang joy, as surely as Sam Butcher carried the car jack those ladies needed. You don't have to be famous or important. You don't have to be acclaimed or much sought after. Just be you. Stay true to yourself and those values that keep you grounded in kindness.

Keep looking for the boomerang surprise in your life. Listen for the whirring sound that means it may be getting close. Always stay connected to people and seek out things that bring you joy. Dream with abandon. Pray confidently. But be careful what you pray for—because everything and anything is possible through the power of prayer!

> Give, and it will be given to you. A good measure, pressed down, shaken together and running over, will be poured into your lap. For with the measure you use, it will be measured to you.

LUKE 6:38

Dear Father, I love the way you surprise me with joy. Life is never a tedious treadmill to the one who knows you. Keep me loving people and doing good. I intend to give a full measure to the world as long as I live in it. And I need your joy! Amen.

God's Tear Bottle

Before you can dry another's tears, you too must weep.

Not long ago I went to the doctor, complaining that my eyes hurt. It seems I travel so much that the atmosphere on airplanes tends to dry my tear ducts. The doctor recommended artificial tears to moisturize my eyes. I laughed, amazed that I would have to buy artificial tears in a bottle, when for years I couldn't stop them from flowing! Those were the days when I took great comfort in the Scripture that assures us God collects our tears in *his* bottle (Ps. 56:8 KJV).

Frederick Buechner said, "Whenever you find tears in your eyes, especially unexpected tears, it is well to pay close attention." Why then do we so often battle our tears and struggle to keep them at bay? One woman describes tearful episodes as a freight train arriving at the wrong time and place or as outlaws shouting, "It's a holdup!" She feels ambushed by her tears.

Even on happy occasions tears can take us by surprise or make us feel ashamed. Many of us cry at happy endings, at weddings and graduations, or at the successful outcomes of traumatic events. But some scientists claim there is no such thing as tears of happiness. They claim we cry not because we are feeling positive emotions but just the opposite. They explain it takes enormous energy to repress our tears. Then, seeing the happiness of others, pent-up sadness and anxiety are discharged. In life, happy endings are the exception, and when one occurs, it stirs up anxieties about the past, they say. The experts claim that each of us is selfish and demanding, that when we cry at weddings, we are really crying for our own contrasting unhappiness. We cry because the real world isn't as happy as the one we want to see.

I'm not sure I agree, because I believe the world is shaped by the hand of a loving God. The Bible shows that we are an Easter people living in a Good Friday world, not Good Friday people living in an Easter world. That means we are destined for joy no matter how difficult our daily life. Something in us responds to the happiness others experience, because we glimpse life as God intends it to be! It is an image imprinted in the spirit of Easter morning—pure, powerful, and potent, like the Resurrection.

So go out there and help create all the happy endings you can. Don't be afraid of tears—your own or those of neighbors, family, friends, or strangers. You will have your share of Good Fridays, but Easter will come. Remember, moist eyes are good. Trembling lips are acceptable. Quivering voices won't hurt anybody. Though tears may disorient some people or send others running for cover, they communicate without words. They are signals that there is something deeper to be understood.

If you are crying, it is a sign that your heart is still tender. If your heart has been broken, you can be thankful that it is still beating and that your feelings have not been shut off. When a song or a book moves you to tears, be glad that the writer has expanded your emotional universe. If you are shedding tears of anger or even hatred, the tears are lubricating, softening your rage. Don't let anyone or anything rip off your tender heart. It is one of the most precious resources you have. Go ahead, feel deeply and let the tears flow. But know too that the blue of heaven is far bigger than gray clouds beneath.

Let your life be rich in tears: tears of compassion when you see a malnourished child suffering on TV; tears of sadness when someone you love is ill; tears of fear and hurt, physical or emotional; tears when you are disappointed, in despair, disillusioned. Let tears of regret, renewal, and rejoicing flow. And don't forget that the most efficient water power in the world is a child's tears. Even crocodile tears! (Where did that expression come from, anyway?)

What kinds of things move you to tears? Are you crying right now? Remember, your tears are precious to God. They are like stained glass windows in the darkness, whose true beauty is revealed only when there is a light within.

Jesus wept.

JOHN 11:35

Father, sometimes I am so close to tears and afraid to let them out. Sometimes they flow and flow and I wish I could stop, but I cannot. From now on I will let them be a sign to me that you are very near. Amen.

Gotcha!

Keep your chin up, and you'll bang your head
on the door frame.

Why don't we hear more about humor in the Bible? Have you ever seen those pictures of Jesus with his head thrown back, smiling so broadly that you can almost hear his laughter? I think those who know the Bible best probably have the most developed sense of humor. Like Billy Graham's wife, Ruth, who grew up in the mission field. Before they were married, she once disguised herself as a frumpy old lady to flirt with him on their college campus. Was Billy ever surprised when she pulled off her disguise and cried, "Gotcha!"

I loved reading Erma Bombeck. She was right up my alley, laughing over things I could relate to, like this: "One exercise program has you doing entire routines while cleaning house. It sounded so simple to bend over my vacuum cleaner and extend my right leg straight behind me while I touched my head to my knee. That was just before the vacuum sucked up my nightgown, causing me to nearly pass out!"

Life never fails to getcha. The best advice in order to face each day is this: Hope for the best, get ready for the worst, and then take whatever God sends. What happens when life is going great and then — whammo! — some big problem hits you, knocking you into a deep valley? You can cheer yourself with the thought that the richest soil is there, because that's where the fertilizer is. Try to find the funny even in the midst of a fiasco. Keep alive the enduring hope that somewhere ahead is a blessing waiting just for you. Picture Jesus throwing his head back in laughter as he anticipates what he has in store for you. The apostle Paul said to think on things that are true, noble, just, pure, lovely, of good report. He wrote, "If there is any virtue and if there is anything praiseworthy — meditate on these things . . . and the God of peace will be with you" (Phil. 4:8–9 NKJV).

Develop a windshield wiper in your mind to slosh off the bad thoughts that splash across your life. Keep driving, and you will move right out from under the cloud that shadows your life.

Yes, life can getcha — when you least expect it. But think of Mary Magdalene's face when she realized that the man who spoke her name in the garden was actually Jesus. She had seen him die, watched his blood run down the cross, brought spices to his grave. Suddenly there he was, talking to her! A huge smile must have spread like sunlight across his face. Surely that moment was the greatest gotcha in history.

If you've watched something or someone you love pass away, take my word for it, *you will laugh again*. Hold on to your hope. Be open and anticipate a good future. The worst grave of all is that of a closed heart. And remember that turning toward laughter is always a right turn, for the sound of laughter is a sign of God's hand upon a troubled world!

> But he knows the way that I take; when he has tested me, I will come forth as gold.
>
> JOB 23:10

Dear God, I see you smiling today. And in spite of the trials and troubles in my life right now, I see you laughing. Knowing that you see what I do not, I don't ask for success, just the simple strength to appreciate your timing and your testing. I know you love me madly, gladly. Amen.

Prayer As Ointment

A lot of kneeling keeps one in good standing.

Prayer is the place where burdens are shifted. Have you ever experienced the joy of coming alongside Jesus, lining up your shoulder next to his? He puts an arm around you, pulling you close. He speaks words of life into your ears, supporting your back under the stuff you are carrying. By the end of the trail you realize the stuff has shifted. It doesn't seem so heavy anymore. Surprised, you look up to see that Jesus has gone on ahead of you, with the heaviest part of your burden squarely atop his shoulders.

For the most part, life is anything but easy. It's like an ice-cream cone—just when you think you've got it licked, it drips all over you. One expert in successful living advises you to simply put your head under a pillow and scream whenever the going gets tough. But I prefer these words of advice: "Blessed are the flexible, for they shall not be bent out of shape!" Prayer is the ointment that keeps our spirits flexible and malleable in the hands of God. Use this ointment before bedtime, and you won't have to muffle that scream.

A little boy captured this truth in an essay on God.

God's second most important job is listening to prayers. An awful lot of this goes on, as some people, like preachers, pray other times besides bedtime. . . . God sees everything and hears everything and is everywhere. Which keeps him pretty busy. So you shouldn't go wasting his time by going over your parents' heads and asking for something they said you couldn't have.

Jesus helps out by listening to prayers and seeing which things are important for God to take care of and which ones he can take care of himself without having to bother God. You can pray anytime you want and they are sure to hear you, because they've got it worked out so one of them is on duty all the time.

God is always on duty in the temple of your heart, his home. You needn't be stiff and formal when you pray. Simply make yourself cozy in the old rocking chair of trust, pulling the afghan of faith around you, and then talk to God. It is the place where Someone takes your trouble and changes it into his treasure.

Sometimes you will find new hope bubbling to the surface. It's like watching the sunrise after a long night. But even if it's still dark when you finish praying, God is with you, reminding you that he cares. Stay in prayer. He will throw another piece of wood on the fire and pull you closer. Resist the urge to complain, because, as someone has said, the more you complain, the longer God lets you live. So pack up your gloomees in a great big box, then sit on the lid and *praise* the Lord who loves you.

God is offering himself to you daily at a generous exchange rate: his forgiveness for your sins, his joy for your grief, his love for your loneliness. You will grow rich as you spend time with him, listening for his voice.

"You wonder whether I understand your trouble?" he asks. "Just watch. You can't turn back the clock, but I can certainly wind it up again!"

"You ask for showers of blessing?" he asks. "Just watch, and don't forget to carry your umbrella!"

Prayer is reaching out to touch Someone — namely, your Creator. In the process he touches you. But prayer isn't magic. Jesus himself did not come to make our suffering disappear in an instant. Instead he came to fill it with his presence. Christians are a lot like pianos — they might be square, grand, or upright, but they are no good to anyone unless they are in tune. To stay in tune with Jesus, follow his call to pray (Matt. 6:6). He promises that our Father, who sees in secret, will repay us as we do. Perhaps the Father will also *replay* us, bringing out harmonies, orchestrating magnificent chords from our suffering, making our lives a new song.

Tell God your needs and remember to thank him for his answers. Prayer is a long-term investment, one that will increase your sense of security because God is your protector. Keep at it every day, for prayer is the key of the day and the bolt of the evening. God is waiting to hear from you.

> But when you pray, go into your room, close the door and pray.
>
> MATTHEW 6:6

Heavenly Father, thank you for the gift of prayer. Forgive me when I don't keep in touch, allowing you to tune my life. Right now I lay myself, my duties, my burdens, small and large, at your feet. In exchange I receive your love and faith. Make me a fine-tuned instrument of your peace. Amen.

Heir-Conditioning

Children aren't happy with nothing to ignore,
And that's what parents were created for.

Motherhood: If it were going to be easy, it never would have started with something called *labor*. Kids can certainly test your patience — and your sense of order too. In a last-ditch effort to save her home from total chaos, one mother resorted to putting little reminder notes all over her house.

Inside the refrigerator: "There is no known sea green food. If noticed, please remove it before it walks away."

In the bedrooms: "Having to make your beds is not considered child abuse."

On the dryer: "Match every sock with something; color or pattern not important."

In the family room: "Items of clothing do not have wheels. They must be carried (to your closets)."

In the bathroom: "Flushing is an equal opportunity job; please press firmly on lever."

On the tub: "Brand-new studies reveal that soap, when submerged in water, will dissolve!"

Parenting is relentless. We keep waiting for it to get easier, but it doesn't. If you are a parent afflicted with hardening of the attitudes, certain you're *always* right, you will identify with the mother who searched a Hall-mark store for the "I told you so!" card section. If you've assumed the role of Grand Potentate over the years, it's time to abdicate. Ask yourself, *Will my being right actually change the course of history?* Take a giant leap and admit the obvious: It's wrong to always be right. Children do not care how much you know until they know how much you care.

When things are bad between you and your children, take comfort in the thought that things could be even worse. Believe me, I know! And when they *are* worse, find hope in the fact that things can only get better. This parenting business is tough. For stress relief now, take a little nap or a long walk. And keep your sense of humor handy—like a needle and thread, it will patch up so many things!

Kids are always learning, from everything you *aren't* trying to teach. They learn, for example, that after a kid stops believing in Santa Claus, a kid gets underwear for Christmas. Resist the temptation to argue. Listen to your kids and learn what's really on their minds.

Remember that patience is the ability to idle your motor when you feel like stripping your gears. Being a parent also means working without a net. Even if you're scared to death, you have to keep going, looking straight ahead and always looking up. Try to brighten *up* a room, polish *up* the silver, and lock *up* the house while your kids work *up* appetites, think *up* excuses, and stir *up* trouble. Before you had them, you believed the old saying that children brighten up a home. Now you know they do, because they never turn off the lights! There is nothing more secure for either parent or child than knowing and loving the heavenly Father above. Now that's a real picker-upper!

When you decided to become a mother, you gave your heart permission to forever walk around outside your body. When that little wiggling child was placed in your arms, you knew nothing would ever be the same again. As kids change and grow, come and go, just keep the hearth fires burning. And remember that mothers should be like quilts, keeping kids warm without smothering them.

For their part, kids are like sponges—they absorb all your strength and leave you limp, but give them a squeeze and you get it all back! And let's face it: Child rearing is a pretty cool job—the biggest "heir-conditioning" job ever!

> Do not forget the things your eyes have seen or let them slip from your heart as long as you live. Teach them to your children and to their children after them.
>
> DEUTERONOMY 4:9

God, you've given me these beautiful gifts—my kids! They are so maddeningly sweet and confusing, lovable and irritating, smart and foolish, all at the same time! Show me how to raise them in you, to always find a way back to you. Thank you for the joy and the trials too. I love them (and you). Amen.

Season of Joy

Each day comes bearing its gifts.
Our part is to untie the ribbons.

Christmas shopping! When do you start this annual chore? I know women who begin the day after Christmas. They buy up decorations and other holiday supplies for better than half price and scour picked-over racks and shelves for gifts. They make crafts all through the winter, hiding them away for the next year. Their Christmas preparations are complete by the beginning of summer! And they enjoy December with their families beside a cozy fireplace.

Other people finally make it to the largest mall in town by mid-December. They wouldn't miss the hurly-burly mood of holiday shopping, including bell-ringing Santas and brightly decorated windows. Then there are those who don't manage to get their cards mailed before Ground Hog Day! If by a miracle they do get it done before Christmas Eve, they triumphantly announce, "This is the earliest I've ever been late!"

Wouldn't you love to simplify the season by finding one gift perfect for everybody on your list? Something personal and practical that doesn't need dusting, can be used immediately, fits perfectly, and lasts forever and a day? One lady said she found it: gift certificates for a flu shot! Another lady gave her weight-watching friends a hand-lettered list of advantages to being chubby during the holidays.

You don't need padding for your Santa suit.
You don't need as much water to fill your bath.
You don't have to buy your clothes in the rap music department.
And there's so much more of you to love!

How they all must have appreciated that!

For many people the holidays are not so jolly. Everybody knows Christmas is supposed to be the season of joy. But it doesn't always feel like it. Do visions of holiday celebrations fill your heart with warm anticipation — or dread? Even for the best of families, all may not be calm and bright. The pressure of expectations, our own and others', often sets us up for disappointment and stress that can sabotage our joy. We remember our losses most keenly during such times of traditional celebration.

Holidays are full of contradictions, and it's okay if our celebrations are too. Our rituals and traditions express good feelings and sad feelings, but they still enhance our family life. Being real about what we feel helps everybody heal. Since women are the holiday ritual makers, it's good to keep this in mind. Your Christmas doesn't have to look like something out of *Victoria* magazine or a Norman Rockwell painting.

Perhaps it will be closer to a painting by Thomas Kinkade. In his paintings light streams from the windows of cozy cottages or churches onto the world outside. He never lets us peek inside, so we don't know what's happening behind closed doors. We only know that the people who live there are living in the light. And we see that light spreading beyond their walls, like an invitation to warmth and fun.

Picture-perfect images? Nothing has to be the way you grew up thinking it should be! Don't feel that this Christmas you have to do everything you've always done, the way you've always done it. Each year create one or two new traditions; try to find ideas that suit your family better than things you did the year before. Encourage the voices, opinions, and wishes of your children, no matter how young. Go for family feeling but keep it simple. What makes your children laugh? Warms the heart of your spouse? Tickles your fancy? The best things are not expensive. The best things come from the heart.

As Christians, we know the reason for the season. Bethlehem's stable was the first step in God's love journey to Calvary's cross. Jesus came in winter, when the world was at its darkest, to a people living under the heel of a cruel Roman Empire. Welcoming that Christmas baby into such a place and time must have taken faith on Mary and Joseph's part. Jesus came bringing his own joy when the world had none to spare. He came shining his own light.

There is always a light in the darkness. Look for it; believe in it. The love of God is shining through the darkest night, brighter than a Kinkade painting. Then get ready for Christmas. Look into the Father's face, tell him you receive his gift, and then untie the ribbons!

In him was life, and that life was the light of men.
JOHN 1:4

-ᚖ-

Dear Lord, your love is like a fire. It brings warmth, light, and peace to my dark places. Your fire both energizes and settles my spirit. By its glow I snuggle closer to you. Thank you for your Christmas gift. One day we will celebrate forever, and there will be no tears, only forever joy! Amen. Come soon, Lord Jesus!

Hug-a-Day Club

Hugging is a miracle drug; look for an overworked,
overdrawn, overlooked, overwrought
(but basically fun) person and give 'em a squeeze!

A hug can relieve tension, improve blood flow, reduce stress, boost self-esteem, and generate goodwill. Hugs cure a lot more than whatever ails you. They keep you immune to illness of the mind. A hug is a tranquilizer with no side effects. What else? A hug requires no batteries, is nontaxable, nonpolluting, extremely personal, fully returnable, and available at absolutely no cost! (P.S.: It is recommended for ages one to one hundred—and up.)

Give hugs away, and you're likely to get one back. But like it or not, sometimes you have to give yourself a hug! One lady I read about was planning a romantic evening the day her husband returned from a hunting trip. As he was unpacking his bag in the bedroom, she heard him say, "Oh, baby, did I miss you!" Turning around to embrace him, she saw he was kissing the remote control! I saw a cartoon recently in which the wife was saying there are times when she can't hold her husband long enough—because she knew if she let go, he would go straight for the remote! Fortunately, self-hugs are not hard to practice. Just wrap those beautiful arms around yourself, give your back a little pat, and squeeze tight. Believe me, it works wonders!

Hugs go together with heartprints. Whatever you do that is compassionate, kind, comforting, or affectionate is a heartprint. Even if it isn't Valentine's Day, a smacka-roo on the cheek might do a loved one good. An arm around someone's shoulder. A firm handshake. A kiss on the tips of the toes. A hand to hold. A full body squeeze. A tear dried with your fingertips. A playful tickle.

How many ways can you bring the touch of God's love to another person? God created us to need the touch of others. Scientists claim that normal people can feel on their fingertips or cheeks something that weighs as little as a bee's wing falling from less than half an inch away! If that is true, we are sensitive to the gentlest gestures. Each stroke registers in our brains, connecting us to a positive experience in the world. But imagine feeling only rude or harsh touches: bumps, jabs, slaps, pinches, pokes, or scrapes. That kind of touch makes you feel irri-table, unsafe, even angry. And what of those who are rarely touched at all? They end up feeling invisible and are invalidated. One woman said, "I've gone to look for myself. If I should return before I get back, keep me here!" Now that is loneliness. She needs a great big hug.

The best exercise for a good relationship is to bend toward somebody else, extend your arms, and pull him or her close to you. God has "everlasting arms." When he said, "It is not good for man to be alone," I think he was thinking of hugs. Every kid should learn that life is full of hugs! It is easy to wrap a hug around a little one, because they are small and squishy. But be sure to squeeze softly. There is nobody who doesn't need a hug—even teen-agers need 'em regularly, although they might need to be reminded to hug you back! You might say, "I think I need a hug . . . and also a maid, a cook, a chauffeur . . . and a lot more hugs!"

Some say the best way to forget your troubles is to wear tight shoes, but I say go out and hug somebody. A day without a hug is too heavy a load for anyone to carry. Sometimes a grouch needs a hug the most! It may be the sunshine that finally drives winter from his or her face.

If you get a hug, enjoy it. And when you leave for the day, always take your hug with you!

His left arm is under my head, and his right arm embraces me.

SONG OF SONGS 2:6

Heavenly Father, thank you for the hugs you give me through the love of family and friends. When I feel alone, remind me that the only equipment I need is my own two arms to hug someone who is even lonelier than I am. Amen.

Scrapbooks of the Soul

I am better than I was but not quite so good as
I was before I got worse.

Scrapbook lovers rejoice! This is your moment! Now you can put together scrapbook photo albums with stickers, stamps, and special acid-free, photo-friendly paper to commemorate life's most important moments. Your one-of-a-kind album will become a family heirloom if you take advantage of special pens, glues, photo corners, mats, page protectors, fun paper punches, and decorative-edged scissors! As for me, I love the idea of finding fresh and creative ways to treasure the moments.

Like Mary, the mother of Jesus, I have treasured many moments in my heart, special memories of God's faithfulness to my family over many years. God himself has used all kinds of colorful and creative ways to document his love, glorify himself, and pass on the heritage of faith through the scrapbook pages of my life. Best of all, he guarantees that none of it will fade away. It is all acid free!

God uses something even better than stamps, stickers, and scissors. He uses that little bottle of magic stuff called Wite-Out! You know, the stuff that does a fantastic job of erasing mistakes. With a dab of a brush, the wrong thing is covered over, leaving a fresh white space upon which he may write.

Years ago when I worked in an office, I called Wite-Out my 1 John 1:9 stuff because it would blot out the mess and leave a clean place—just like God does with our sins. We all need spiritual Wite-Out to make us white as snow (Isa. 1:18). We can all have a clean, fresh start every day. God no longer sees our sin because it is covered by his special Wite-Out: the blood of Jesus.

In our journey through life, the scraps and souvenirs we save can be turned into artwork by the creative hand of the Lord. Let him sit down at the table of your life and go to work. And while you're at it, why not help him out? Gather up all the color you can. Cut away the broken ends of your life. Find "stickers of the heart"—things to make you laugh. Most of all, don't let the best you have done so far be the standard for the future. You can do even better. Let God use his Wite-Out; it works wonders!

> If we confess our sins, he is faithful and just and will forgive us our sins and purify us from all unrighteousness.
>
> 1 John 1:9

Almighty God, my Redeemer, thank you that the blood of Jesus cleanses me from my sin. Please send your Holy Spirit to fill me with your peace so I can rest in the midst of my circumstances. You have given me for-giveness and righteousness in Jesus' name. Hooray for your heavenly Wite-Out! Amen.

Living at Geriatric Junction

My bifocals are adequate, my dentures fit fine.
My face-lift is holding, but I sure miss my mind!

We all know why God made it so difficult for women over fifty to have babies, don't we? Why, they would put them down someplace and forget where they left them! Of course, I only forget three things: names, faces, and . . . oh dear, I forgot the third!

Men are just as bad, I guess. They forget names and faces, not to mention birthdays and anniversaries. Later on they forget to pull their zippers up, and even later they forget to pull them down! If that isn't bad enough, think of their hair problems. The reason men don't need face-lifts is because sooner or later their face will grow right up through their hair. One man I talked to said when he was young he used to wash his hair with Head and Shoulders but now he uses Mop and Glow. A friend of mine who is completely bald refuses to wear turtlenecks, certain they would make him look like a roll-on deodorant! Here's a cure for baldness you might want to try: Mix one part Epsom salts to one part alum mixed with three tablespoons persimmon juice. Vigorously rub this mixture into your husband's scalp three times daily. It won't keep his hair from falling out, but it will shrink his head to fit the hair he has left!

One lady wrote about problems her husband was having as he grew older: "He's been doing dumb things," she said. "While I was away visiting my sister, he did the laundry by stuffing his dirty socks into water glasses, then putting them in the dishwasher. Then he wore the socks and drank out of the water glasses." (I warned this lady to stop visiting her sister and stick close to home.)

Another lady told me her husband just sat around with the remote in his hand. I comforted her with words I once heard someone say: "If you love something, set it free. If it returns, you haven't lost it. If it disappears, it wasn't truly yours to begin with. If it sits there watching television, unaware it's been set free, you probably already married it!"

To aging women who worry about the passing years, I say, "Just relax and enjoy life, even the parts you can't remember!" After all, the only way to look younger is not to be born so soon! It's impossible to fool Mother Nature, no matter how much you exercise — especially when all you exercise is *caution*.

An old-timer, of course, is anyone who learned to ride a bicycle before it became a fitness machine. My middle-aged girlfriend started an aerobics program but quit because her thighs kept rubbing together and setting her pantyhose on fire! As for me, whenever I think about exercise, I lie down until the thought goes away. My idea of strenuous exercise is to fill the bathtub and lie back, then pull the plug and fight the current. How's that for maturity?

Nowadays most of us are a lot like ducks swimming in a lake — composed on the surface but paddling like crazy underneath. Real maturity, we discover, means being gentle with the young, compassionate with the elderly, and tolerant of the weak as well as the strong —

because we have been all these things at one time or another. The best way to grow in maturity is to pray this little prayer every day:

> Thank you, dear God, for all you have given me, for all you have taken from me, for all you have left me!

I spoke recently at a retreat for "golden-agers," folks between seventy and eighty years old. Breakfast was to be served buffet style, with each table of ten going up for food. The table with the folks taking the most pills that morning would get to go first. That was the prize! With *seventy-two* pills (Bill and I had already taken ours in our room), our table took the honors.

As we grow older, pills and all, we need to carve out happiness and joy every day. But we can't do it by avoiding things. Trying to stave off age or trouble is like trying to nail Jell-O to a tree. We can only do it by entrusting more of ourselves to God each day.

One nice thing about the passing of years is that you and your children eventually wind up on the same side of the generation gap. You can avenge yourself on them by living long enough to cause them trouble. Another nice thing about aging is that each day you get closer to seeing the Lord. Imagine that scene! To me it has a silvery sheen; all sadness is transformed and everything dull will be made bright!

Reynolds Wrap celebrated its fiftieth anniversary last year. The salesman who sold the first roll of aluminum foil is still alive at age eighty-four. In fifty years Reynolds produced seventy-nine million miles of the stuff, enough to stretch from the earth to the moon and back 180 times! Something about that picture reminds me of God's silvery stuff stretching from heaven to earth many times over—

wrapping us in his protective love as the years pass. Because of that I'm not afraid of aging, forgetfulness, pills, or creaky bones. I just remember that growing old is mandatory but growing up is optional. I am always in my prime until I get wrinkles in my heart!

> For a thousand years in your sight are like a day that has just gone by, or like a watch in the night. . . . Teach us to number our days aright, that we may gain a heart of wisdom.

PSALM 90:4, 12

Dear God, keep me unafraid of passing years. They go so quickly! I place my life in your love. I am hid with Christ in you. Bless this body of mine and use it to bless others as long as possible. Amen.

Just a Little Hope

Hope is a wonderful thing—one little nibble
will keep a man fishing all day.

"When a neighbor needs help, you just give it, knowing it's the right thing to do." That's what one woman said when a twister struck her small town. Hundreds of people whose homes had been spared reached out to help less fortunate neighbors.

In another town a single mom was told she had only thirty days to buy the house she lived in; otherwise she would be evicted. Suddenly her dreams for her family were dashed. On the other side of town another woman felt an urge to call that very day just to say hello. That one call changed both their lives forever. "It was apparent she had been crying," the caller later explained, "so she told me about the eviction. I knew that what happened to them could happen to any one of us." A simple plan was hatched that day to save the family's home.

You never know who needs a bit of human kindness *right now*. A note or letter of encouragement may be all that is needed. If you feel the urge to reach out, don't procrastinate, because tomorrow may be too late.

One woman went to her doctor to get the results of a checkup. The doctor said, "I have good news and bad news. Which do you want first?"

She answered, "The good news!"

The doctor said, "You have twenty-four hours to live."

"Good grief," exclaimed the woman. "That's the *good* news? Then what's the *bad* news?"

"The bad news," replied the doctor, "is that I was supposed to tell you yesterday."

Even able-bodied, self-sufficient people treasure small gestures of kindness. Proverbs 12:25 says, "An anxious heart weighs a man down, but a kind word cheers him up." You might write a card recalling a sweet memory you once shared with someone going through a hard time. You might remind a sick friend of how their own past kindness can strengthen them now. Or you might simply list all the positive qualities of a son or daughter or spouse. If you hate to write, clip out stories and cartoons, or pop a few autumn leaves or pressed flowers into an envelope and mail them to a friend. Make a special meal for someone who is hurting. Join a bake sale — and remember that charity is when you make cookies for a worthy cause; compassion is when you buy them back.

Nowadays we are so busy, it's hard to find time to do something thoughtful. You have to slice the time from your schedule. If you do, encouragement will come boomeranging into your own backyard! One of Sweden's past queens once sold her jewels to build hospitals and orphanages throughout the country. Years later as she visited one of these places, tears from a bedridden woman fell glistening onto the queen's hand. She exclaimed, "God is sending me back my jewels!"

Paul wrote: "I urge you . . . to offer your bodies as living sacrifices, holy and pleasing to God" (Rom. 12:1). Now, we all know that the problem with being a living sacrifice is that it's so easy to crawl off the altar. Don't do it. Commit yourself to being a hope bringer no matter what. Hope looks for the good in people, opens doors for people, discovers what can be done to help, lights a candle, does not yield to cynicism. Hope sets people free.

A gracious word may smooth the way,

A joyous word may make one's day!

I recently read about a survey in which ninety-five-year-olds were asked, "If you could live your life over, what would you do differently?" The old people mentioned two things: "We would reflect more" and "We would do more things that would last beyond our lifetime."

Don't let your life speed out of control. Live intentionally. Do something today that will last beyond your lifetime. People can live for up to seventy days without food, ten days without water, and six minutes without air. But they can't live without hope. Be grateful today for the hope you've been given and then find creative ways to pass it on to someone else.

> Because of the LORD's great love we are not consumed, for his compassions never fail. They are new every morning.
>
> LAMENTATIONS 3:22–23

Our heavenly Father, thank you for being the source of everything worth living for. Give me ideas and energy to bring your kind of hope into the lives of the people around me. And thank you for its boomerang effect! Amen.

Dream Big

May your day be fashioned with joy, sprinkled with dreams,
and touched by the miracle of love.

Allow your dreams a place in your prayers and plans. God-given dreams can help you move into the future he is preparing for you. A little girl once wrote on her science paper, "When you breathe, you *inspire*. When you do not breathe, you *expire*." Dreaming should be as natural as breathing. But who among us hasn't suffered from a broken dream or two? When that happens, we suffer a kind of spiritual death and need to surrender our lost dream to Christ, asking him either to restore it or to give us a brand-new one.

Even daydreams can be gifts of God, so it's important to pay attention to them. Experts claim they can reveal things that help us organize our time, develop our goals, and cope with our problems. Taking a few moments to daydream can also calm, relax, and give you perspective.

The psalmists frequently focused on peaceful images. Psalm 23 speaks of quiet waters, a sumptuous table, and green pastures. Thinking about such a place must have quieted David's spirit and strengthened his faith. Even the image of the dark valley was redeemed by the image of God walking through it beside him. This kind of daydreaming renews. "He restoreth my soul," wrote David (Ps. 23:3 KJV).

Close your eyes right now and use every one of your senses to dwell on thoughts that bring you closer to God. You might start by reading the last chapter of Revelation, which is filled with amazing mental images of the great things God has in store for those who love him. These are God's special dreams for his children.

As you dream, keep in mind these ABCs.

Aim high.
Believe in God.
Consider your options.
Don't give up.
Enrich your soul.
Find faith in doubt.
Go for the grace.
Hang on.
Ignore discouragement.
Just let Jesus!
Keep trying.
Love life.
Make merry.
Never say, "I can't."
Open your mind.
Pray hard.
Quit whining.
Read the Bible.
Stay strong.
Take on the challenge.
Understand the obstacles.
Value virtue.
Wait patiently.
X-ccelerate hope.
Yield to the Holy Spirit.
Zero in on joy.

Today pray over your dreams, asking for God's blessing and guidance. Then write them down in the form of goals and seal them in an envelope. Entrust it to a friend, asking that it be returned to you in one year. Meanwhile whenever these dreams cross your mind, think about them with faith and enthusiasm and commit them to the Lord. Take whatever steps he invites you to take, but don't worry about feverishly pursuing them, because this will only rob you of energy. Thank God for his way of making those dreams come true.

Still, there will be obstacles. When trouble assaults your dreams, think TICDAABGC — Things I Can't Do Anything About But God Can! Make a list of all these things and then post the list on your bathroom mirror. Add items as necessary. Now affirm your commitment to God's love, life, and laughter. Wake up each morning with faith on your lips and tuck yourself into bed each evening in faith's comforting blankets. God can take the sour, bitter things in your life and blend them into something that smells and tastes as sweet as honey. Generate enthusiasm wherever you go; it will power your dreams!

There are three kinds of people in this world: those who make things happen, those who watch things happen, and those who don't know what on earth is happening. Which kind will you be? Paul wrote, "Forgetting those things which are behind, and reaching forth unto those things which are before, I press toward the mark for the prize" (Phil. 3:13–14 KJV).

Don't you want to inspire others like that? I do. I will do my best with what I have as long as I am able. A student once wrote, "Dew is formed on leaves when the sun shines down on them and makes them perspire." The heat of life may make me sweat, but it is going to be given back to the world as shining dewdrops.

Ambition is sometimes a negative word, connoting overblown egos and ruthless self-promotion. But when ambition means dreaming God's big dreams for your life, it's another matter. Here's my prayer for you as you head for your dreams: May the Lord bless thee and keepeth thee going!

He who overcomes will inherit all this, and I will be his God and he will be my son.

REVELATION 21:7

Dear Lord, so many dreams, so little time! What am I to do? Guide me and lead me, even if it means only taking one small step after another. I will give you free reign in my life to do your will, thankful I am your child. Amen.

Merrymaking

I'm not fifty—I'm eighteen
with thirty-two years of experience!

This year many Americans will turn fifty. But fifty ain't what it used to be. Judith Jamison, artistic director and ballet choreographer, says, "What's nice about being fifty is the beat, the rhythm, the movement. Nobody's stopped." The tennis great Billie Jean King adds, "I think fifty now is what thirty-five used to be. Spiritually and emotionally you get stronger."

I never wrote a word until I was fifty years old. Now I have three million books in print in twenty-four languages, plus braille and large print. My publishers are as flabbergasted as I am, because I have never even attended a writing seminar. That just shows how God can use you even when you're living between estrogen and death. I like to remind myself that time is merely what keeps everything from happening at once. Have you heard about the seven stages of womanhood?

In your twenties you want to wake up with romance.
In your thirties you want to wake up married.
At forty you want to wake up rich.
At fifty, to wake up successful.
At sixty, to wake up contented.
At seventy, to wake up healthy.
And at eighty you just want to wake up!

Smack-dab in the middle, the fifties are a time of metamorphosis. When short hemlines came back into fashion, one woman dug a miniskirt out of a box at the back of her closet and tried it on. It looked great—except she couldn't figure out what to do with the other leg!

Some say that life is a test, that if it were the real thing, we would have received further instructions! But think again, because we have the Bible, the greatest instruction book of all! The Bible is a love story wherein God encourages us to make our lives meaningful. But more than 45 percent of all men, and 40 percent of women, say they are "still trying to figure out the meaning and purpose" of their lives. However, only 28 percent of women over age fifty say they are still trying to figure it out. So age on, girls—the best is yet to be! You know you're getting close to real maturity, by the way, when you are content to feel right about something without needing to prove another person wrong. Or as someone else said, when you progress from cocksureness into thoughtful uncertainty.

A doctor recorded the complaints of some of his midlife patients. One woman complained of feeling "lustless." Another woman requested a "monogram." He heard about "migrating" headaches and "mental-pause." But even menopause is not an ending but a pause—a time to regroup before making a fresh start. Gather your energy. Redefine your goals. Be glad for a change. Medical researchers say women get a surge of mental, spiritual, and physical energy after menopause. So get ready. Get set. Go! And remember that each day is like a suitcase—every person gets the same size, but some people figure out how to pack more into theirs.

I always set aside the first day of every month to do something fun just for myself. Opening mail, cooking, and household chores are off-limits. Sometimes I try a new hairstyle or sit down in my favorite chair and go catalog shopping. Once I drove to a high bluff overlooking the freeway, parked, put on an inspirational music tape, and just watched all the activity below. The first of every month is my time to renew my soul.

Maybe your schedule doesn't allow you to take a whole day for yourself, but you can spend part of a day doing something fun: fly a kite, walk on the beach, pack a yummy lunch and find a special place to eat it. Enjoying yourself doesn't have to be expensive. You can do something I call "merrymaking" anytime, anywhere. That's when you express your joy over small successes — like the time that awful stain came out of your dress, or your checkbook actually balanced.

Life is short. Each year passes more quickly than the previous one. It's easy to deny yourself many of life's simple pleasures because you want to be practical. Forget about practical and decide instead to become a joy collector. Always be on the lookout for gifts without ribbons. God is strewing them across your path right now. His gifts come tagged with a note: "Life can be wonderful. Do your best not to miss it!" Enjoy what is before it isn't anymore.

God will scatter surprise blessings across your path in the next few years. Don't be like the woman who described herself as passive and bored, a "mush melon living in a middle-aged frame." Instead be zany and giddy. Dare to slip on a pair of bunny slippers once in a while! Surprise yourself! Enjoy the little things because one day you'll look back and realize they were the big things!

> For the kingdom of God is not a matter of eating and drinking, but of righteousness, peace and joy in the Holy Spirit. . . . Let us therefore make every effort to do what leads to peace and to mutual edification.
>
> ROMANS 14:17, 19

Dear God, you help me see I don't need to get stuck in a midlife crisis. Instead I want to step enthusiastically into your kingdom life. No more blahs, bummies, or battles with gloom. I am waking up to your great world, great people, and a great future. Thank you for rolling out the red carpet as I turn fifty. Amen!

Blessed by Stress

Somewhere over the rainbow—that's where the airline
will find my luggage.

I'm not kidding. Even stress can be a blessing if you
know how to deal with it. I first entered "the school of
stress" during my teenage years when I attended a pri-
vate Christian high school in the Deep South. As soon as
I arrived, I saw a large sign: GRIPING NOT TOLERATED.
(Hmmm. In my family *griping* meant throwing up! I figured I could try not to throw up while I was at school.)
Then I saw signs over the doors of every room in the
school; signs like: DO RIGHT and DON'T SACRIFICE THE PER-
MANENT ON THE ALTAR OF THE IMMEDIATE. You get the idea.
This school was very big on The Rules.

How could I possibly live according to all these rules
every day? I thought it might just kill me. But it didn't.
Instead of bucking the system, I did everything I could
to cooperate. I learned then that there is a whole new
way to react to things you do not like. When you go
through a whole semester telling yourself, *I will not gripe,*
not griping not only becomes a positive habit, it elevates
your attitude.

Of course, it was exhausting trying to be so good all the
time. But eventually I discovered that the real trick to
dealing with stress is to kick it out of gear, roll with the
punches, and take one day at a time. Instead of asking

God to get rid of it, I had to learn to neutralize its effect. I discovered that winners turn stress into something good, while losers let stress turn life into something bad. Winners see an answer for every problem, while losers see a problem for every answer. Knowing these differences and incorporating them into the way you face stress is key to keeping your dignity and peace in adversity.

Some people just can't seem to get the hang of it. A friend wrote, "Barbara, I tried relaxing, but somehow I feel more comfortable being tense." Changing our patterned responses to life can be uncomfortable but well worth it.

A woman named Anna Mary Robertson refused to resign herself to the stress of aging. After rearing ten children and despite being plagued with arthritis in her hands, she took up painting. Twenty-five percent of her work was completed after she had turned one hundred years old! We know her as Grandma Moses, the gifted artist who produced more than fifteen hundred sought after paintings.

Another elderly woman modeled stress reduction based on her love of the Bible, especially Psalm 91:4, which reads, "He will cover you with his feathers." Whenever this lady experienced stress, she would repeat to herself, "I am covered with feathers. I am covered with feathers." One night while walking down a dark street, she realized she was being followed by two men. Fearful, she began to affirm out loud, "I am covered with feathers! I am covered with feathers!"

One of the would-be muggers shouted, "Hey, man, this lady is crazy. Let's get out of here!" And they fled!

Emily Dickinson wrote, "Hope is the thing with feathers that perches in the soul." It's a wonder Paul didn't include feathers in the armor of God, described in the book of Ephesians. Paul tells us we need to be fully clothed in order to fend off the fiery darts of our Enemy. Yet too many of us are like Christian streakers. We put on the helmet of salvation but forget about the rest of our armor. To beat stress, we also need the belt of truth, the breastplate of righteousness, the shoes of readiness to share God's peace, and the shield of faith. Oh, and let's not forget about the feathers!

The truth is that every day has its share of stress. When you feel like an aerosol can because you are under too much pressure, find a listening ear to act as a safety valve. Throw a pity party for your friends so you can all get it out of your system at once. Drown your fears in compassion for each other and then rise up and give yourselves a great big hug. Encourage each other to hang on and hang in there! As Launa Herrmann says, "If you keep hanging in there, your wrists won't stretch, but your adaptability will!"

I've come to believe that big crosses — every once in a while — work to our advantage, for they teach us to bear the little ones calmly. What about tomorrow? Let God worry about it! It belongs to him.

A righteous man may have many troubles, but the LORD delivers him from them all.

PSALM 34:19

Lord, I don't want to corner the market on stress. I am doing the best I can to let it go. I pray for light and love along the path, enough to see me through. I know you are there for me every step of the way. Amen.

Women of Faith partners with various Christian
organizations, including Zondervan,
Campus Crusade for Christ International,
Crossings Book Club, Integrity Music,
International Bible Society,
Partnerships, Inc., and World Vision
to provide spiritual resources for women.

For more information about Women of Faith
or to register for one of our nationwide conferences,
call 1-800-49-FAITH.

www.women-of-faith.com